OVER *the* CIRCUMSTANCES

Jan Ellis

Over the Circumstances
Jan Ellis

Published September 2020
Express Editions
Imprint of Jan-Carol Publishing, Inc.
All rights reserved
Cover Photo: © Shock / Adobe Stock
Copyright © 2020 Jan Ellis

This book may not be reproduced in whole or part, in any manner whatsoever without written permission, with the exception of brief quotations within book reviews or articles.

ISBN: 978-1-950895-56-4
Library of Congress Control Number: 2020945462

You may contact the publisher:
Jan-Carol Publishing, Inc.
PO Box 701
Johnson City, TN 37605
publisher@jancarolpublishing.com
jancarolpublishing.com

*I dedicate this book to God,
who, through the sacrifice of His Son
and the inspiration of His Holy Spirit,
gives me the insight to share.*

Contents

Foreword vii

Author's Preface..viii

Why *Over the Circumstances?*..1

Who is Jan Ellis? 4

Taking the Mystery out of Hearing the Voice of God....................7

How God Speaks to Us 9

Theme 1: The Word of God – The Foundation of It All Us............20

Theme 2: Becoming His – Learning to Let Him Be Lord 29

Theme 3: Intimacy with God – Knowing and Being Known...........37

Theme 4: Prayer – Just Talking to Your Father..............................60

Theme 5: Faith and Trust: Experiencing Real Peace 71

Theme 6: Guidance and Direction: Walking in Confidence 82

Theme 7: Spiritual Maturity – Growing into Your Purpose.............94

Theme 8: Ministry – Walking out Your Destiny............................115

Theme 9: Relationships with Others 135

Theme 10: Difficulties 145

Theme 11: Dealing with Being Human 164

Final Thoughts..201

Acknowledgments...207

Foreword

By Pastor Michael Booker

Jan is an outstanding child of God. She is a faithful, committed servant and has a heart to help others know the Lord. This book is fantastic and will help you in your walk with the Lord. Your heart will explode with information as she shares how to hear God speaking to you in your everyday life. I highly recommend this incredible book for anyone who wants to get closer to the Lord and to hear Him speak to you and guide your life.

By Pastor Scott Emerine

Jan Ellis is an insightful writer and servant of God who beautifully blends her stories in a vivid way that helps readers connect with what she is writing. God has taken her through some unique situations during her life's journey, but she has carefully crafted short stories in a way that breaks down the Word in an entertaining and informative way. She has faithfully served at Covenant Fellowship alongside her husband, Paul Ellis, for years and has become a great friend. She has touched countless lives through her life and ministry, and this book will do the same.

Preface

My List of Disclaimers:

1. This book is not a devotional. Several regular readers of my blog suggested I should write a book of devotional pieces. I can see why they thought my blog posts would lend themselves to that type of writing. Each piece is short, has a lesson, and often includes Scripture.

    I didn't want to write a devotional because I know how badly I fail at keeping up the discipline of reading a book designed for daily reading. Every time I commit to reading through such a book, something comes up that makes me miss a day. Then I feel like I must "cram" to catch up, and it becomes a legalistic chore. I didn't even make the number of chapters or essays a nice round number like 30, 60, or 90, so you shouldn't feel like you must finish reading it in a month or two or three.

2. If you have ever read my blog, you may recognize many pieces. The hardest part of working on this book was reserving content that God was giving me until I could publish it. When I received inspiration for writing one of my articles, my first impulse was always to put it on the blog. There's also some new material for those of you who have been loyal blog readers. Even if you've read some of this before, I hope that the second reading will

bless you again or show you something you might have missed the first time.

3. The final disclaimer: I am not perfect. I'm not even sure I would consider myself mature in the Lord. The lessons He shows me sometimes must be repeated in many different presentations before I fully understand and put them into practice. I'm still growing, as we all are, and I do not consider myself to be a perfect example of a Christian.

The subtitle of my blog says, "I've decided to live *over* my circumstances instead of under them. Follow my journey and see where God takes us." That's the point of putting these thoughts in this one book. Let's learn something together.

All scripture references in this book are from the New King James Version (NKJV) unless otherwise indicated.

OVER *the* CIRCUMSTANCES

Why *Over the Circumstances?*

You might be wondering where the blog and book title *Over the Circumstances* originated. One influence was something that I heard long ago from a former pastor of mine. Davy Jo Hissom was an amazing man of God with a great sense of humor, and he lived life with joy. He often said that when he asked people how they were doing, they would answer, "I'm doing okay under the circumstances," to which he would reply, "Well, what're you doin' under them things?" Then he'd always say that he knew that phrase wasn't good English but that he wasn't teaching English!

He was right. God designed us to live a life that is victorious regardless of what is happening around us and to experience a joy that is not dependent on the current situation. The Bible calls us *overcomers*, not *underdogs*.

"Who is he who overcomes the world, but he who believes that Jesus is the Son of God" (1 John 5:5)?

"Yet in all these things we are more than conquerors through Him who loved us" (Romans 8:37).

I also chose this title because it's a lesson I have learned from my own life. I had a happy childhood—secure in the love of my parents, embroiled in typical sibling rivalry with my sister, Brenda, raised to know God, and blessed to have many material advantages and unique experiences. I enjoyed good health, did well in school, and had good friends. Then, within the space of fewer than three years, I lost both my mother and my father to cancer. Later, because of my own choices in life, I became a single mother. That situation put me in a position of financial and emotional difficulty for quite some time. Even marrying a good man of God did not insulate me from pain and problems. We have had our share of those, as most people have experienced. Once, someone remarked that they thought I'd had a hard life. It took me by surprise because even with all the events that I have listed, I've never really felt that my life was hard. I know others who have struggled with as much or more than I have. I simply thought of all of that as just… life.

When the amazing love of God chased me down and brought me back into a relationship with Him, I began to learn the lessons of how to experience joy in the middle of adverse circumstances. A relationship with God puts all things into perspective, and I began to see that the day-to-day events of my life are not all there is to my life. God has a plan I cannot begin to understand, but He teaches me through everything that happens in my life—both the things I can control and those for which I am not responsible.

I'm not saying I spend every minute of every day walking on clouds or that I never feel sad or disappointed; it's just that I'm not on an emotional roller coaster anymore. I find the key in these words: **"And we know that all things work together for good to those who love God, to those who are the called according to His purpose" (Romans 8:28).** If I am "the called" according to His purpose, and I pursue my calling first, then I don't have to be concerned about all the little things that happen day-to-day. I know that ultimately, God will use those things to accomplish what He has planned for my life.

"For our light affliction, which is but for a moment, is working for us a far more exceeding and eternal weight of glory…"(2 Corinthians 4:17). Sometimes the things that try our faith are the very things that are building us up to be more effective Kingdom people. If walking according to our calling is our primary focus, then this is what we should desire.

I wish I could say I'm always the perfect model of faith regardless of the circumstances in which I find myself. I'm not. However, I have found that when I remember this principle in the middle of all that life throws at me, that is when I am most content. I've also walked through situations where God has made Himself very real to me precisely because of what I am experiencing, and while I would never want problems, I would rather have Him in the situation than never know Him at all. I have issues, but the issues don't have to have me.

Who is Jan Ellis?

As you read this book, it may help to have a little knowledge about my life and "circumstances" to help you understand the background of some of the stories. My parents raised me in a stable home in a small town in West Virginia. I went to church and Sunday School, but until my early teens, Jesus was just like a cartoon figure on the Sunday School lesson paper. He wasn't real to me at all. He was more like Santa Claus or the Easter Bunny—an invisible character that I'd never met.

Then our church took part in a program where Christians from other churches across our state came and spent a weekend meeting with small groups of people from our church to share their faith and get our folks talking about their relationships with God. Though most of us probably thought we were Christians, we were just going through a lot of religious formalities, rituals, and customs without really knowing the God we were worshipping. This encounter tremendously impacted our church and our family. My family soon became involved in visiting other churches and sharing our faith as members of those ministry teams.

However, even though I wanted to love and serve God, I was wrapped up in a lot of insecurity. I looked like the poster child for the "good daughter" and "the girl most likely to succeed," but internally, I was a mess. My mother died of cancer in October of my senior year of high school, and I felt more adrift than ever without her steadying hand in my life.

Eventually, I sought validation in relationships with boys, and eventually men, who made me feel desired and beautiful, not realizing they were preying upon my weaknesses for their purposes. I became pregnant and dropped out of college when I was just barely into my second semester. I gave birth to my daughter, Nikki, in October of 1978. My father died only six months after she was born.

I went back to college and earned a teaching degree, and on the surface I looked like I was back on my feet, that my life had been set back on course. In some ways it had. I was employed as a teacher and made a home for myself and my daughter, but those insecurities still led me into destructive relationships. Craving stability and security, I sought them in a man, but nobody was able to provide that for me.

Finally, in the late 1980s, I visited a church where the pastor was a young evangelist whom I had heard speak in my college town before I left there to take my first teaching position. I can't tell you what he preached that night. I only knew that I was at the lowest point I had ever been in my life. I was a wreck, mentally, emotionally, physically, and spiritually. I went to the altar that night and never looked back. I sat under the teaching of this man, Davy Jo Hissom, for just eight months before a plane crash took his life. During those brief months, I learned more about the Bible, my relationship with God, Christian living, and destiny and purpose than I'd ever learned in my life.

With that new, strong foundation, I began to find my identity, stability, and security. I was right: I had been looking for those things in a man, and I'd found them in a man. His name was Jesus. I remember praying one day, "God, I don't care anymore if I ever get married. I am so content in You that if a single life is what You want for me, then that's fine."

Of course, with God's sense of humor, when I quit looking for a mate, He sent one to me. My husband, Paul, and I started as friends in the church's singles' group. I held him at arm's length for a long time and tried to keep him as "just a friend," but then I learned that friendship was a strong basis for a relationship, much better than the drama of my previous romances. I finally surrendered to the inevitable. On July 18, 1987, we were married. Paul adopted Nikki, and two years later, our son, Josh, was born.

Fast forward—we now live in Bristol, VA. My daughter is happily single and lives in West Virginia. My son is married to my daughter-in-law, Brittney, and they have an adopted daughter, Bella, who is the light of my life. During these 30 plus years of marriage, we have lived in West Virginia, Florida, and Virginia, and at this writing, our house is the 21st home we've shared. We are members of a remarkable church called Covenant Fellowship, and we are still pursuing the God who changed everything.

So that's the cast of characters that you'll hear more about throughout the book. My family gives me a lot of insights, and I don't think there would even be a blog or a book without all the things that Bella teaches me just by growing up.

That's the set of circumstances I'm "over" right now. They are mostly good, but there are challenges in every life. You'll hear more about them later. Right now, let's get to the good part: What is God saying?

Taking the Mystery Out of Hearing the Voice of God

Many people have said to me, "God just doesn't talk to me." I think maybe He does, but they just haven't learned to recognize His voice.

My husband and I have been married for over 30 years. After thousands of conversations and many years of shared experiences and intimacy, he can be three aisles away from me at Walmart, and I can tell it is him just from the sound of him clearing his throat! That kind of familiarity is born of a serious investment of time.

I believe that the more time we spend with the Lord in prayer and in meditating on His Word, the more we will recognize His voice. I also think that, because His relationship with each one of us is unique, we won't all experience His voice in the same way. For me His voice comes through like giant capital letters in my mind—a clear, pure thought without any other "mental clutter" of my own thoughts. You may hear Him in a much different way, but He will communicate with His children.

"Then you will call upon Me and go and pray to Me, and I will listen to you. And you will seek me and find Me, when you search for Me with all your heart" (Jeremiah 29:12-13).

To me this verse says that I will find God to the extent of the intensity with which I pursue Him. I don't know about you, but I want to be so close to Him that I can recognize Him merely by the sound of Him clearing His throat!

How God Speaks to Us

We are all unique beings, created by a God who knows us intimately and loves us unconditionally. He knows how we learn, how we respond, what kinds of things we notice, and what we enjoy. If He wants to get a message to you, He can find the right channel. If, and only if, you are tuned in to His frequency, you can receive what He is trying to communicate to you. The prerequisite for that "tuning in" is that you are born again.

"But the natural man does not receive the things of the Spirit of God, for they are foolishness to him; nor can he know them, because they are spiritually discerned" (1 Corinthians 2:14).

It's a little like a foreign language. You may know a few words of Spanish, which allows you to pick out an occasional phrase in a native speaker's conversation, but you won't understand the whole meaning of the message, as you are not speaking the same language. Much of what Christians discuss can sound foolish to the rest of the world because the unsaved don't have the basis for understanding. They might think they know what God is saying, but without a relationship with Him, they cannot truly understand.

When humans communicate with each other, they use many different methods. We talk to each other in a give-and-take exchange that can take the form of a face-to-face conversation, a chat on the telephone, or an internet connection. We can also speak to others in one-way communication, like a video or audio recording.

Written messages can be handwritten or typed and then handed or mailed to someone. (Remember passing notes in school? Are any of you that old?) We text, email, write Facebook posts, and blog.

The arts can be a way of relating ideas through song, dance, movies, art, or photography. Artists' thoughts and emotions are visible in their creations. Keystrokes on a virtual page reveal the souls of writers. Inventors touch and change the world with their witty inventions. Even just a touch or a look can transmit a world of information. Our actions are said to speak louder than words.

<u>If we as humans can communicate in so many ways, how much more creative is our God?</u>

My granddaughter, Bella, is fascinated by watching me put on makeup, because her mother doesn't use cosmetics. Every time she is with me when I'm getting ready to go out, she wants to sit on the bathroom counter and observe me. She also wishes I would doll her up a little, too, which I do by hovering my makeup brushes just above her already beautiful complexion, so she doesn't end up with much of anything on her face, but Bella thinks she looks fantastic.

One day I had just opened a new jar of moisturizer. As I prepared to put some on my face, she stuck a tiny finger in the opening and plunged it to the bottom of the container. I pulled her finger out and rescued the product on her hands. However, that little tunnel made by her finger remains in the jar as of this writing. Every time I open that jar, I see that indentation, and I smile at the memories of our girly time together. She's left an imprint on something she has touched.

Every time we interact with people, we leave some sort of impression. When we touch physical objects, we leave a tangible print.

God created the universe, so He has also left His fingerprints on every inch of it. The structure of things, the processes, the interrelationships between objects, the reactions when different substances come together—all of that has a natural purpose. Still, I believe that, because He touched those creations, He has left hidden lessons within them that are for us to seek out and discover. **"It is the glory of God to conceal a matter, But the glory of kings is to search out a matter" (Proverbs 25:2).**

You may not feel very royal, but this verse says, **"...Grace to you and peace from Him who is and who was, and who is to come, and from the seven Spirits who are before His throne, and from Jesus Christ, the faithful witness, the firstborn from the dead, and the ruler over the kings of the earth. To Him who loved us and washed us from our sins in His own blood, and has made us kings and priests to His God and Father, to Him be glory and dominion forever and ever. Amen" (Revelation 1:4-6).**

Because He loved us and saved us, He has made us kings and priests, and therefore it is in the realm of possibility that we can search out a matter that He has given to us to explore.

God talks to me through the things I observe in the areas with which I am most familiar. I see connections in my interactions with my family, my students, and my friends. Items and processes in my home sometimes bring a spiritual lesson to me. Perhaps you are a nurse or doctor, an engineer, a mathematician, a gardener, a construction worker. You can see lessons and spiritual parallels in situations where I would not, because you understand the inner workings of the things you are observing in a way I don't comprehend.

The Holy Spirit used me once in an exhortation to my church family, and He said, "I'm talking all the time. Listen! Listen!" I have never heard the audible voice of God, though some people have. God is not limited to the use of our ears. You may be familiar with some of the ways that He has spoken to me because you've experienced them in your life, but God may use many other tools to speak to you. I hope that reading this book will help you to tune in, listen, and hear what He says to you and then share it with others.

Before you seize on any thought, impression, idea, dream, or insight as coming from God, make sure it agrees with the sources of authority He has given us: The Holy Spirit and the Word of God.

Jesus said this about the Holy Spirit: **"But the Helper, the Holy Spirit, whom the Father will send in My name, He will teach you all things, and bring to your remembrance all things that I said to you" (John 14:26).** Any insight that comes through any of these stories is His wisdom, not mine. Someone complimented a recent blog post, and my response was, "Thanks! God sets it up; I just record it," and that's how it works for me.

God gave us His Word, the Bible. Its authority and truth govern all other ideas that we think God is sending to us. If it doesn't line up with the Word of God, it's not from God. He will not violate His own Word. **Psalms 89:34 says, "My covenant I will not break, Nor alter the word that has gone out of My lips" (Psalms 89:34).**

1. The Bible — Reading What He Wrote

This one may seem like a no-brainer, but I'm not talking about regular, systematic Bible study here. I'm also not referring to the method where you just open the Bible randomly and point to a verse in the middle of the page for guidance. (I do not recommend that method at all. It can have very misleading results.) What I mean is that there are times when I'm reading something in the Bible that I may have read dozens of times before, and suddenly, the words seem to, as many people say, "leap off the page at me." These are times when God makes a verse relevant in an extraordinary way that gives me guidance or insight into a situation.

Here's one example of this. One evening I was reading in Exodus. It says, **"So Moses spoke thus to the children of Israel; but they did not heed Moses, because of anguish of spirit and cruel bondage" (Exodus 6:9).**

As I thought about this verse, I realized that God had told Moses to tell the people of Israel that He would release them from their bondage, be their God, and give them a land of their own. However, they did not listen to or believe these magnificent promises, because they were too focused on their emotions (anguish of spirit) and their circumstances (cruel bondage).

If I had just read the words "anguish of spirit" and "cruel bondage," I might have just read on through the story, but when the Holy Spirit did the translation in my mind to "emotions" and "circumstances," I could better see what He was trying to teach me in that moment. I needed to focus on the promises of God rather than how I felt and what circumstances I could see. The Apostle Paul wrote about Moses and the children of Israel: **"Now all these things happened to them as examples, and they were written for our admonition, upon whom the ends of the ages have come" (1 Corinthians 10:11).** How can these examples impact us if we don't see what we have in common with the people with whom God is dealing in the Bible? If you let the Holy Spirit be your teacher, He can give insight into how a specific Scripture applies to you.

2. Thoughts — Listening When He Speaks

Everyone thinks. Not all thoughts are "God-thoughts." I'm sure you can agree if you know anything about your own thought life. However, sometimes when I am praying about a specific situation, I get this thought that is very "to the point" and clear. The words seem stamped on my consciousness like giant capital letters.

The first time this ever happened, I was 16 years old. I was in my bedroom praying about some situations in the lives of other people. I don't remember the specifics of those prayers now, but I know they were issues that were heavy on my heart. In the middle of all my petitions to God, I distinctly "heard" Him say, "Praise Me!" I argued with Him for a moment. "But, God, there are all these problems. How can I praise you?" Again, I heard, "Praise Me!" This time I was smart enough to obey Him, and I began to lay those things aside and concentrate on praising Him. What followed was one of the most exciting times of prayer and intimacy with God that I had ever experienced in my life.

The Word says, **"...in everything give thanks; for this is the will of God in Christ Jesus for you"** (1 Thessalonians 5:18). Notice that it doesn't say to give thanks *for* everything but *in* everything. He is worthy of praise, thanks, and adoration regardless of our life circumstances, and there is power in that praise.

3. Object Lessons — Seeing What He Shows

I have been a public-school teacher for more than 30 years. I think my love for teaching goes back to the third grade. Because of some overcrowding in the school building that served grades one through twelve, our third-grade class met in a small rented building within sight of the official school building. I suppose that our teacher didn't get a planning period because we were not with other school personnel, so she often gave me the job of calling out the words for a spelling bee, as she knew that I could read them all. That gave her some time to grade papers and plan lessons.

As I got a little older, I did 4-H projects dealing with childcare. I also did some babysitting, and as a teenager I taught a children's Sunday School class. Instead of just talking to the children or reading the Sunday School lesson from the curriculum, I looked for object lessons, which were ways to illustrate a Biblical principle with objects that could be observed with the eyes or touched with their hands. The classic object lesson is showing the concept of the Trinity (Father, Son, and Holy Spirit) by breaking a raw egg. The egg consists of a shell, yolk, and white, yet all are still one "egg," just as all the Persons of the Trinity are one God.

Jesus used this type of lesson in many of His parables. He used the ordinary objects and situations of His surroundings and turned them into stories the people would understand. As you go through the motions of your daily life, ask the Holy Spirit to show you the parallels between those mundane events and processes to give you a better understanding of spiritual truths.

4. Dreams — Interpreting What He Sends

I am a prolific dreamer. Every single night of my life, I have vivid dreams. I am always right in the middle of one when my alarm shatters my sleep. Though I don't immediately understand their messages, I try to write them down so I can refer to them as I learn more and as God gives me more insight and resources to help me see what He is trying to say.

God used dreams to speak to people throughout the Bible. He gave direction to Joseph to take Mary and Jesus to Egypt to protect them from Herod. Daniel received prophetic dreams. **"'And it shall come to pass in the last days, says God, That I will pour out of My Spirit on all flesh; Your sons and your daughters shall prophesy, Your young men shall see visions, Your old men shall dream dreams"** (Acts 2:17).

The book of Job says, **"For God may speak in one way, or in another, Yet man does not perceive it. In a dream, in a vision of the night, When deep sleep falls upon men, While slumbering on their beds..."** (Job 33:14-15).

Of course, dreams should be interpreted prayerfully and cautiously and viewed through the authority of God's Word first.

I've never dreamed the same dream twice, but there is a common theme in many of them. I am usually doing a walk-through of an empty house that I'm either purchasing or have just rented when I discover rooms that I didn't know were there when I first toured the property. The homes are never the same, and the circumstances aren't identical, but that common thread of undiscovered rooms is always there. After prayer and talking to others who are skilled in Biblical dream interpretation, I realize that those new rooms are new opportunities in my life—places in my spiritual journey, natural life, and ministry that I have not yet walked. Since I began recording these dreams in 2009, many of those opportunities have opened to me, and I believe there are more to come.

5. Children — Looking in a Mirror

Working with children as I do every day, there are many things I see that can have an application to my life. My granddaughter is my favorite teacher. Almost every time I am with her, God shows me something in her growth and development that mirrors a spiritual issue with which I am dealing.

You'll read many "Bella" stories in this book. When we are together, God quickens my spirit to recognize my behaviors and attitudes in what she says and does. I guess, in some ways, I am a spiritual toddler!

Here's an example: Bella was warned by her mother to stop doing something or else punishment was coming. Bella's attempt to save herself was classic: "But my papaw loves me!" He was miles away in his own house, oblivious to her situation, but she thought that because of his love, her parents shouldn't punish her! Aren't you glad you have a Father who isn't far away who knows your situation and has already provided a way of escape from the punishment you deserve?

6. Our Brothers and Sisters in Christ — Hearing Wise Counsel

Sometimes God uses a person in our lives to dispense His wisdom to us. Have you ever been listening to a sermon when the speaker suddenly seems to almost fade away into the background as his words begin to penetrate your spirit with a direct message from God? My current pastor, Michael Booker, says that we should listen to the Voice behind the voice. As he receives direction from the Holy Spirit on what our local church body needs to hear, he shares it with us, much like I just record the lessons God is teaching me.

Other times God can speak through individuals who can impart a word to us that is very personal and on time. Once, I was struggling with a disappointing outcome when Paul and I tried to get financing to buy a home in the Abingdon and Bristol, Virginia, area. We had a couple of other financial blows the same week, and I was tired and discouraged. I doubted my ability to pray and to hear from God. We made an appointment to meet with Pastor Michael, and the words I received from him were not at all what I had expected. I think I was anticipating sympathy, but his words were a combination of gentle rebuke mixed with some comfort. He reminded me that the enemy was going to fight the spiritual giftings I was beginning to discover in my life, and in pulling back from God in my disappointment, I was giving the enemy exactly what he was seeking. His words encouraged and challenged me to walk in a renewed commitment to press on and trust God.

Just a couple of months later, I was sitting in a church service, and for some reason I kept glancing at a young woman sitting to my left in the next section. I knew her name but not much else about her. The

Holy Spirit just kept speaking the same phrase in my mind over and over. After the service I took another strong woman of God with me to talk to this young woman, and I gave her this phrase, "'Let It Go' is not just a song in a Disney movie." I had no idea what that might mean to her, and evidently, she didn't either! She looked at me like I had two heads.

Later that afternoon this same young lady called several other people in the church to track down my phone number so she could tell me her story. At that time we were having two Sunday morning church services. The encounter I had with her was during the first service. She didn't understand the words that I'd said to her that morning, but as she was exiting the sanctuary that morning, she encountered someone who was entering the room for the second service. This man was a former pastor of hers who had wounded her deeply by accusing her of some immoral actions of which she was not guilty. She had left his church a long time before. Later he was caught in some compromising situations himself and was no longer leading a church. She said she realized the moment she saw his face that the Holy Spirit was telling her to "let it go" and forgive him. The anger and pain dissolved in the act of forgiveness. The entire story still gives me "Holy Ghost goosebumps." God uses others to speak to us, and He can use us to get a message to them. Amazing! I'm so glad I listened so that she didn't miss the freedom God was trying to give her.

* * *

When God speaks in your life, through whatever means He uses, it's an incredible experience. One of the things I've been doing for several years is writing down these lessons and events in a journal. When things are difficult, it's been such a blessing to be able to pick up this little book and read about the faithfulness of God in every facet of my life. I can encourage myself by remembering where I have been and looking forward to where I am going.

The remainder of this book is a collection of many of these types of lessons grouped in themes. Because they are in themes, they are not in chronological order. I've listed my granddaughter's age if she is the subject, so you can picture a typical child of that age as it applies to the story. Please enjoy them and glean what you can from them. I hope they are a blessing to your life.

Theme 1:
The Word of God —
The Foundation of It All

Fingers on the Right Keys — Starting from a Position of Truth

I was typing some sermon notes one night, and I glanced away from the screen for a few seconds. When I looked again at what I had written, it seemed as if I'd stopped typing in English and begun recording notes in some foreign language! Evidently, my fingers had moved one place to the left. They had carried on typing in the correct pattern but with the wrong letters, causing an incomprehensible jumble of unpronounceable syllables on the screen.

When you start from the wrong position in life, it has a profound effect on the things you think, the opinions you hold, and the principles on which you base your life choices. You may have firm convictions about specific issues, and you think you can justify them. You just keep on churning out ideas in the way you speak and the way you live, but unless those things are rooted in the only real truth that exists, all your rhetoric is just as foolish and nonsensical as my typed gibberish.

Our world today is full of many opinions. It seems that everyone is always arguing about politics and religion, morals and values, judgment and mercy. Even in the church world, there is shocking compromise and a rejection of the very Word of God by people who think they are more loving and compassionate than God. They change the gospel to fit the culture instead of letting the Jesus of the gospel transform the culture. There is one constant in all the changing landscapes of our civilization, and it's not pop culture, the media, or anyone's opinion. It's the authority of an Almighty God who doesn't need to "get with the times" or update His Word to fit modern sensibilities. When we start thinking that we know better than our Creator, we've got our fingers on the wrong keys, and everything that we say or do beginning in that position is flawed.

The thing that everyone seems to be missing is this: it's not that God set down some arbitrary rules so that He could be in charge and make everyone toe the line *or else*. It's the fact that He designed us, and He knows what will bring us the greatest fulfillment in our lives and what will cause our lives to be a blessing to others rather than a heartache. He's a loving Father who could control every aspect of our lives but instead allows us the choice to accept or reject His plan.

No matter how intelligent someone is by the world's way of measuring intelligence, he or she is no match for God. The arguments that begin by setting man in a position as more "with it" than the God who created him are just babble and nonsense.

The book of Timothy talks about the people of God praying for all men and expresses God's heart about truth and how He views it. It says, **"...who desires all men to be saved and to come to the knowledge of the truth" (1 Timothy 2:4).** Please note that this verse uses the phrase "the truth." It doesn't say "one of the many truths" or "your truth," as the world says these days. He loves us, and He knows that only *His* truth will set us free.

Whose Truth Sets You Free?

It amazes me that in a cynical, sinful world that is scornful about the things of God, I frequently hear snippets of Biblical sayings in television shows, movies, and songs and see quotes in books and articles. I hear God's name and the name of Jesus spoken, not necessarily always in vain. Characters will even "pray" after a fashion, asking questions of God or asking God to help them in a situation.

I heard one such reference the other day in a television drama. The main character learned the real story of an event from her teenage years, and in that new knowledge, she had to face something she didn't want to know about a family member. She, as the narrator in this scene, said, "They say the truth sets you free," and continued talking about what she had learned.

"And you shall know the truth, and the truth shall make you free" (John 8:32).

"Jesus said to him, 'I am the way, the truth, and the life. No one comes to the Father except through me" (John 14:6).

But "the truth" that she was referring to was not the same as Jesus being "the truth." Truth is not just facts, or a motto that you live by, or even a scripture. Truth is a Person.

Truth is more than a set of principles. It's more than a body of knowledge. All the principles and knowledge in the world cannot free you from the mess that you, being human, have created. Facts can't forgive your sin, free you from your bondage, or guide your future. All facts can do is contribute to your human reasoning. I think we all realize how fallible that can be.

Jesus is the Truth, not a truth, or one of the truths, but THE TRUTH. Yes, He will use the "truths" in His Word to mold and shape us, but the first truth we must know is that He is THE entry point. We must consider all the facts, mottos, and Scriptures through Him first before they can make any sense in our lives.

You've probably heard people in the media talking about "Living Your Truth" like it's some sort of new religion, and, in a way, I guess it is. The enemy has twisted and manipulated the truth from the beginning of time. These lies have created a maze of ideas and creeds and slogans and lifestyles. Many people are now in total mental confusion. Our own "truth" is flawed from the beginning, and trying to live it leaves us just stewing in the same cesspool in which we've always immersed ourselves.

The quote saying, "Christianity isn't a religion; it's a relationship," may be overused, but it's undoubtedly not over-experienced. Even those who go to a church that is considered a Christian denomination may still never have actually met "The Truth" or had their lives changed by Him.

It doesn't take much to see that the world needs the absolute truth, because each of us living by our own set of truths is causing nothing but pain, stress, conflict, and foolishness. I don't know how many times in the last few years I've either heard or said, "The world's gone crazy." We all need the only actual truth that has ever existed: Jesus.

Brainwashed

"I don't understand people who aren't me. They're weird!"

If you imagine that last word said with a high-pitched whine (in two syllables), you can put yourself right at the scene. Those were my husband's words to me this morning. My husband is known for his wisecracking remarks, but I think he was only half kidding about this one.

Sometimes it is difficult to hear all the wide-ranging opinions of others on issues—such as gun control, gender confusion, religion, politics, and the subject of the week on Facebook—and not feel like the entire world (except you) has gone crazy. We are all sure we are right about everything, or else we wouldn't think what we think.

So what should our standard be for how we think about all these things? It's a simple answer but not an easy or instant thing to do. The Word says, **"And do not be conformed to this world, but be transformed by the renewing of your mind, that you may prove what is that good and acceptable and perfect will of God"** (Romans 12:2).

When there is no perfect standard for what is right, then confusion reigns. The Apostle Paul put it this way: **"These things we also speak, not in words which man's wisdom teaches but which the Holy Spirit teaches, comparing spiritual things with spiritual. But the natural man does not receive the things of the Spirit of God, for they are foolishness to him; nor can he know *them*, because they are spiritually discerned. But he who is spiritual judges all things, yet he himself is *rightly* judged by no one. For 'who has known the mind of the Lord that he may instruct Him?' But we have the mind of Christ"** (1 Corinthians 2:13-16).

There is no point in arguing with a natural man about spiritual things. They regard them as foolish things. Until the Holy Spirit breaks through in the life of a person, he or she will not be ready to receive the things of the Spirit. The New Testament term for repent is metanoia, which not only means regret or being remorseful for what we have done, but it also means to have a "change of mind." Only then are we open to truly begin to think as God thinks.

Many unbelievers will say of us, "You Christians are all just brainwashed." Pastor Davy Jo used to say, "Everyone in the world is brainwashed by something or someone. At least I'm choosing who gets to wash my brain!" When we allow outside influences to "wash over us" in what we read and listen to, by who we gather around us, and by what we watch, we give them the power to influence our thinking. I don't know about you, but my brain needed a good scrubbing when

I came to Jesus, and I need to remember to keep renewing my mind in Him.

What if Your Pastor Gave a Test?

All over the United States, states give school children controversial, end-of-the-year, "high stakes" testing. School boards use it to judge the effectiveness of schools, individual teachers, and curriculum. The scores measure children's mastery of the knowledge and application of subject matter.

One complaint that teachers have is that there are lots of variables that influence a student's performance on a single test. Some children are model students but have test anxiety, or they may feel sick on the day of the test. Other students haven't applied themselves all year or have behavior problems and haven't allowed the teacher to help them learn the material. Some students just don't take the test seriously and just choose any answer so they can finish. Test results aren't always an accurate measurement of what a teacher has spent the current school year teaching.

It's not just a matter of memorizing facts, dates, and mathematical procedures; it's a matter of application. For instance, some of my students could tell you that seven multiplied by eight equals fifty-six. However, when faced with a word problem such as, "If Susie had seven baskets with eight apples in each basket, how many apples did she have?" they might add rather than multiply, showing that they know the facts but not when to use them.

I'm not going to debate this issue in this writing, but it got me thinking about the other areas of my life where education is involved, like being in a church where the Word of God is taught and preached. It made me wonder how I would perform if my pastor gave me a test.

What would happen if your pastor gave a test on the content of what he has taught this year? How would it reflect on the church, the pastor, and the Bible itself? Would everyone remember the Scripture references and the points the pastor made? Even if they did, would they be able to demonstrate that they knew how to apply what he had taught to a "real-life," "outside the church walls" situation? Have they gone beyond head knowledge to heart knowledge?

Teachers tell students all the time that they can't master everything they need to know just by attending school. If the only reading they do is in reading class, they won't become fluent readers. That takes practice and study outside of the classroom. Similarly, if the only Word you ever hear is during a Sunday morning service and you never read and study it for yourself, you'll never become proficient and effective in the things of God.

I don't know any pastors who give a written test. They don't have to, because our lives themselves are the test. In my educational history, I was usually a pretty good student, but in my spiritual life, I've not always been so diligent. As a result my "grades" in life have been less than stellar many times. I'm so thankful for the grace of God, which doesn't "grade" us but sees us through the righteousness of Jesus.

I want to fulfill the purpose of God in my life, so I'm making a renewed commitment to be faithful, to meditate on the words I hear from my pastor, to spend time in the Word for myself, and to seek God's help in effectively applying what I learn to my own life. Remember, though, that all the Bible knowledge in the world is nothing without first having a relationship with the Author. I'll try to remember that, too, as I spend time discussing the lessons I learn with my Teacher.

"Be diligent to present yourself approved to God, a worker who does not need to be ashamed, rightly dividing the word of truth" (2 Timothy 2:15).

A Light in the Darkness

I made a grocery store stop one evening to pick up a few odds and ends. As I drove up the hill to the parking lot, something seemed wrong. It took me a minute to realize that the large pole lights in the parking lot were off. Even with my car headlights on, it was difficult to see the painted lines on the lot so that I could maneuver my car into the parking spot correctly.

This incident reminded me that the Bible says God's Word is a lamp unto our feet and a light unto our path. When the light isn't there, you struggle to get where you need to go and to line yourself up in the correct place.

Walking to the store with only the light shining from the store windows made everything feel gloomy and a little frightening. The light makes you feel so much more secure.

"But if we walk in the light as He is in the light, we have fellowship with one another, and the blood of Jesus Christ His Son cleanses us from all sin" (1 John 1:7).

We are beyond blessed to have Jesus and His Word to dispel the gloom and guide us to position ourselves correctly in this life.

Beyond the Obvious

There is a game that I play on my cell phone when I have an idle moment, like when I'm waiting in a doctor's office or when someone is late in starting a meeting. This game gives me just six letters to use to make as many as twelve words in a crossword-style grid, but there are no clues. At first I see the obvious combinations and connect the letters to make the words that stand out to me. Then I try adding suffixes to the words I've made if the correct letters are there to make that attempt. My next strategy is to think of words that rhyme with those I've already formed. Finally, I look at the grid structure and view the hints hidden in the position of the letters in the words that remain.

Many times I will look at the few letters that are presented to me and think, *There is absolutely no way that I can make that many words from this meager amount of letters!* It looks impossible, and I cannot find any meaning in the jumble of letters I see. Eventually, though, with time and reflection, I fill in the entire grid.

I think the Bible is a lot like a word puzzle. Of course, the worth of the Word of God is infinitely more valuable than a time-wasting game, but there are some parallels between the two. At first reading of a passage of Scripture, we can get the surface meaning. We quickly latch on to what is familiar and what we have heard preached and taught before, but if we move on and dismiss this as just that "same old passage" that we've heard a thousand times, we won't see the entire "grid" or structure that God is trying to build in our lives.

Dedicated Bible study is more than just reading. Just like the puzzle, we must look at Scripture beyond the immediate and instant understanding, then find connections and associations between what we are reading and what God has said in the entirety of His Word. We can find application to the current situations in our lives. If we are willing to dig into the Word and ask the Holy Spirit to be our Teacher, we will find treasures that will bring beauty to our lives and the lives of others. Challenge yourself to complete the puzzles in your life with the letters you possess.

Theme 2:
Becoming His/ Learning to Let Him Be Lord

A Joyful Grave

I witnessed a powerful baptism service this morning. Many people were baptized for the first time as they professed their new relationship with Jesus. Others took that plunge in a demonstration of a new commitment after a time of spiritual brokenness. Some people were drawing a symbolic line in the sand to mark a day when things would change in their lives and their ministries. The service went long after the usual time that we dismissed, and I needed a bathroom break! But as we watched the Holy Spirit working so powerfully, my husband leaned over and said to me, "You can't leave the room during a funeral service!"

It took me just a second to adjust to what he was saying, but Colossians says it pretty much that way. **"...buried with him in baptism, in which you also were raised with *Him* through faith in the working of God, who raised Him from the dead"** (Colossians 2:12).

We were watching a series of burials. Old lives, old attitudes, old struggles, and old obstacles were being put away—not just being covered up and ignored, but being healed and transformed.

At the end of the service, we watched the ushers prepare the portable baptistery before moving it. Paul said, "Look, they're putting the lid on the coffin." Another wise observation from my always witty husband. Baptism is a grave where Jesus buries our past. **Romans 6:6 says, "...knowing this, that our old man was crucified with *Him*, that the body of sin might be done away with, that we should no longer be slaves of sin" (Romans 6:6).**

The joy in the house this morning was evident. Jesus is still moving, still changing lives, and still intervening in circumstances. I hope you are in a place where you witness this freedom taking place in those around you, but more than that I pray that freedom and joy are abundant in your own life. If not, maybe it's time to bury some things of your own.

Who Owns Your House?

A person has a far different relationship with a rented house than with one that they have purchased. We were in our last rental for two years. Though I was thankful for that home and appreciated many of its features, it was still not really "mine." When we first moved in, I hung some pictures and arranged some furniture to decorate it, but it was never a place that I had grand dreams of remodeling, because when you rent you don't invest money in making changes to something that doesn't belong to you.

Then God dropped a little thought along those lines into my mind. If a house is a symbol for our own lives, then I wonder how many of us treat God like he's a renter instead of the owner of our "house?"

A renter pays the price to dwell in a home but is not permitted to make decisions about the property and can only make the changes that he clears with the landlord first. If a person treats God as a renter, not as the owner of the house, Jesus would be the person's Savior but not his or her Lord. Jesus has paid the fee on the cross, which should have been enough to purchase the "house" entirely, but once He is in the house, many doors are bolted and padlocked to deny access to Him. "God, you can have this area of my life, but I want to retain control of these other places."

"For if we live, we live to the Lord; and if we die, we die to the Lord. Therefore, whether we live or die, we are the Lord's" (Romans 14:8).

"I have been crucified with Christ; it is no longer I who live, but Christ who lives in me; and the *life* I now live in the flesh I live by faith in the Son of God, who loved me and gave Himself for me" (Galatians 2:20).

Like the rented house, we may dwell here, but we belong to someone else. When we offer our lives entirely to God, our lives become His. We cannot say to a landlord, "This part of your house belongs to me." He owns all of it.

When I own a house, I dream BIG! On a few occasions in my life, I have had the opportunity to make changes to those homes that I have owned. Some were necessary and functional, like putting on a new roof when the current one was leaking or damaged. Some were much more fun, like adding a roof over a section of a back deck to provide a shady place to enjoy the outdoors. Others added beauty to an area, like painting a room a different color or adding pretty new light fixtures.

Just like those improvements, God wants to spend lavishly on us. He can make necessary and functional changes in our lives, like helping us change our attitudes in the middle of our circumstances or helping us forgive someone who has wronged us. The Holy Spirit can make enjoyable changes, like guiding us to discover new things about our gifts and talents that give us opportunities to do things we never imagined. He can bring beauty to our lives through the many blessings

He can provide. He can even enlarge our "house" to show us new possibilities in our lives that will stretch us beyond what we ever dreamed we could experience.

Oh, how much He desires that we would treat Him as Who He is: the One who purchased us and the One who should have full control of our lives, not to impose His will *on* us but to dream *with* us, to plan the remodeling—the great Designer who can show us His vision of what the house can become.

Who Has Life?

The other day I heard a phrase we often use in Christianity. The person speaking said, "I gave my life to the Lord." What he meant was the same thing we all mean when we use those words: we accepted the work that Jesus did on our behalf, acknowledged our sins, asked for forgiveness, and became a new creation in Him—born again.

I've heard the phrase a thousand times, but that day the words struck me a little differently. When you give something to someone, you must possess it in the first place. While we are in the body, I guess, to a certain extent, we own our lives. We are the ones making decisions daily that tell our bodies what to do and what to say, but the "life" we have is nothing we can give to God. He gave us the lives in our mortal bodies so that we can even exist.

When we come into a relationship with Jesus, He gives His life to us, not the other way around!

Life is more than just the absence of physical death. We all have heard of people who seemed to be living "the good life." They had money, position, fame, talent, looks—everything the world thinks is required for happiness—yet they were miserable, and some even took their own lives. I've known others who had little the world would envy, yet the joy that radiated from them was incomprehensible.

The Bible tells us, **"...for in Him we live and move and have our being..."** (Acts 17:28). The life that we have in Jesus is so much more than anything we can gain in the natural world. Jesus Himself said, **"I am the vine, you *are* the branches. He who abides in Me, and I in him, bears much fruit; for without Me you can do nothing"** (John 15:5).

If we do not maintain that connection to Him, we can begin to dry up spiritually. He promised that He would never leave us, but the choice to leave Him can be ours. I have learned that leaving Him doesn't always involve jumping back into the deep end of the sin pool. It can be as simple as ignoring His voice or avoiding his Word. It can just be prioritizing our wants before His will. We will never follow Him perfectly, but we can be pursuing Him in obedience regardless of how we feel or what circumstances surround us. Choose life!

Preparation

As I sit typing this tonight, the sky outside my window is blue with fluffy white clouds. Yet the weather forecast is calling for thunderstorms with high, damaging winds, hail, and a possibility of tornado activity. If I had no access to modern weather reports, I would never expect any such thing based on what I see just outside my house.

The news is advising people to secure items that are outside so that they won't blow away. They say to be watchful of the conditions so we can move our families to safety if the weather worsens. Warnings of fallen trees bringing down powerlines ring in my ears, and in some areas near where I live, the power is already out.

I've prepared just as the warnings advised. In case of a power outage, I'm currently getting a blog post ready to submit, doing a load of laundry so I'll have something to wear to work in the morning, and planning to do some computer work related to my job. Dinner has already been prepared and consumed, and if there's time before it starts storming, I'll have an early bath. Everything I am doing on this Sunday afternoon and evening has been affected by just the possibility of something happening. Maybe it will; perhaps it won't.

At the same time, all around me in this world are people who have not made any preparations for the life they will have after this one. Though they may not believe it, that forecast is a sure thing. Human beings will prepare for vacation, for retirement, for accidents, and for natural disasters, but they pay no attention to the condition of their souls and their eternity.

The signs of the times indicate that it won't be long until Jesus returns for His church. Christians know that prediction is set in stone because God Himself made that forecast. No, we don't know when, but we do know to prepare.

How do we prepare? It's not just by believing facts. The enemy himself knows all the facts. It's a knowing and acting upon this truth that shows that our trust is in Jesus.

Every sports fan has seen the Scripture reference for John 3:16 held up on a sign in the stands. **"For God so loved the world that He gave His only begotten Son, that whoever believes in Him should not perish but have everlasting life" (John 3:16).**

Jesus also said, **"I am the resurrection and the life. He who believes in Me, though he may die, he shall live" (John 11:25).**

There is your preparation, but it's only the beginning. When you believe something with your whole heart, it's not just an intellectual exercise; it's the basis for everything you do and say in life.

Are you prepared? Do you know who holds your future here on earth and your eternity in heaven? Are you ready for the storms to come? I hope that you are. If you watch and listen, you'll begin to see signs of the times and know that it's time to think about these things. I'm going to sign off for tonight and finish my list of preparations for this natural storm, because now I hear the wind beginning to blow.

A Way of Escape

Driving to church one morning, a bug on the inside of the driver's side window was annoying my husband. As we slowed to a stop at a traffic light, he rolled down his window and tried to shoo the bug out into the fresh morning air, but the stubborn creature clung to the edge of the window. He batted at it several times, but it was no use. Finally, in exasperation he squashed it against the window that it seemed so determined to occupy.

My first reaction was, "Ewww!" as I heard the crunch of the bug under his finger. I remarked that he had given the bug plenty of opportunities to escape but that, in rejecting the offer, the bug had chosen his disaster.

In this case the insect's actions had literal life or death consequences, but for us as spiritual beings, the choices put before us are eternal. We can choose a never-ending, joyous home in heaven with God or eternal separation from Him in hell. The bug may not have known about the imminent dangers, but we do. A single choice determines the outcome.

"Nor is there salvation in any other, for there is no other name under heaven given among men by which we must be saved" (Acts 4:12).

However, it's not only the eternal escape that we need; we also need a way to be rescued from the challenge of our sinful nature, still rearing its ugly head in our lives. Fortunately, God has provided a solution to that issue as well.

"No temptation has overtaken you except such is common to man; but God is faithful, who will not allow you to be tempted beyond what you are able, but with the temptation will also make the way of escape, that you may be able to bear *it*" (1 Corinthians 10:13).

I'm so glad that God has mercy toward us and is long-suffering, even waiting many years for some of us to take advantage of that open window into the fresh air of life in Him. Still, as my pastor taught this morning, God has also said that His Spirit would not always strive with man **(Genesis 6:3).** That window of escape that allows you a chance to live, prosper, and find your purpose in this life won't always be there. Take advantage of the unfathomable opportunity God has given you: first to accept His salvation and then to walk with His Spirit, which will rescue you from all the traps and snares the enemy lays for you in this life. It's your choice.

Theme 3:
Intimacy with God — Knowing and Being Known

Hold You
(Bella at 21 months)

In just a few months, our beautiful granddaughter, Bella, will be two years old, and at that point I guess I'll have to stop calling her a baby. Even now she's communicating like a little person and beginning to put a couple of words together to make short phrases. My favorite one is when she is standing at my feet and reaches her little arms up to me and says, "Hold you!" Not hold *me*, but hold *you*.

In my mind asking to be held is communicating a need for comfort or rest, but asking to hold someone else is an expression of wanting to be close to and express love for another person.

Throughout my life there have been many times when I have sought solace in the arms of Jesus. The Holy Spirit is called our Comforter for a reason. But what joy it must bring to His heart when we come to Him just to express our love, when we ask to "hold Him!" God desires to be close to us. He desires intimacy with us. He wants to bring us revelation and insight. The book of Jeremiah says, **"'Call to Me, and I will answer you, and show you great and mighty things, which you**

do not know'" (Jeremiah 33:3). Just like when Bella cries out, "Hold you!" and I scoop her up, when we cry out, God answers.

Amazing Love

When our son was a little boy, he often said to us, "I love you a million thousand every day." Like most parents we remember the cutest things our kids said and still talk about those childish utterances even though those babies are now adults. I loved this phrase so much that I created a wall plaque with those words, which now hangs above my kitchen sink.

One day I was walking through the house, and as I glanced at this plaque, God said to me, "Think about those words a minute, and I'll show you something."

As I meditated on that little boy's declaration, God showed me that when my baby boy said, "a million thousand," he imagined the biggest number he could, indicating the depth of the love he had for us. When he used the words "every day," he meant not just Christmas morning, or the day we took him fishing, or the time we went to an amusement park, but every single ordinary day of his life.

God said, "My love is much the same. A million thousand is only a tiny fraction of the infinite love I have for my children. I love you so much that I gave you Jesus, and your mind can only understand a tiny part of what that means for you. My love for you is every day, not just when you have it all together, not just when you pray exactly right, not just when you've studied the Word or lifted your hands in worship, not just when you are treating those around you in the way you should. I love you on the days when you are broken or doubting, or frustrated, or angry, or unforgiving, or apathetic. I love you deeply and unconditionally."

Every morning when you wake up to start your day, imagine our awesome God greeting you with that phrase: "I love you a million thousand *every day!*"

Delight
(Bella at 1 year)

While my son and his wife were out of town one weekend, my daughter-in-law's sister kept our granddaughter. I volunteered to take her for the last few hours of the time they were gone so her aunt could catch up on any sleep she'd lost over the weekend! Doing so was no great sacrifice for me, because I'm a little crazy about this bundle of joy.

When we arrived at the house, her aunt came to the door carrying the baby, and that sweet little girl's face broke into a huge smile when she saw my husband and me coming through the door. She bounced in her aunt's arms and reached for me, so excited to see us. That brought such delight and joy to my heart. Knowing that she recognizes us and is happy to be with us is an amazing feeling. When she shows such enthusiasm to be with me, it makes me want to bless her with anything her tiny heart wants.

Of course, as many little natural occurrences in my life do, this one made me think of how God relates to all of us. I know that He loves us unconditionally, but can't you just picture the delight and joy that we bring to Him when we are pursuing Him with abandon, when He can see our excitement at spending time with Him? I wonder if God's heart swells like that, making Him just as eager to bless us as my heart is to treat that baby with what will please her.

There are some clues about this in His Word.

"For the eyes of the Lord run to and fro throughout the whole earth, to show himself strong on behalf of *those* whose heart is loyal to Him" (2 Chronicles 16:9).

The end of this verse echoes that. **"For the Lord will again rejoice over you for good as He rejoiced over your fathers"** (Deuteronomy 30:9).

"Delight yourself also in the Lord, And He shall give you the desires of your heart" (Psalms 37:4).

These are just a few of the many examples that show us that God wants a relationship with us and has so much to give us—more than we could ever imagine.

This connection is not an emotion or attitude that we can fake. It is born of a real relationship, just like the one my granddaughter has developed with me in the last year. How did that happen? She is not yet capable of a conversation. She can't read my blog or understand my spoken words. It happened because she was a helpless newborn who received all that her parents and extended family provided for her. We fed and bathed and dressed and kissed and loved and encouraged and celebrated her from the day she came into our lives. She has learned to rely on us for all that she needs. She is learning how to communicate her needs to us by reaching out for the things she wants. We've played silly baby games with her, and she knows what fun is. You should hear that little musical giggle! She has lived with all of us day by day, and she knows us, trusts us, and needs us.

In our relationship with Jesus, we are as helpless as newborns sometimes. We need to receive all that He provides for us. We learn to trust Him for what we need. We learn to communicate our needs in prayer, although our first attempts at those conversations may be clumsy and awkward. As that relationship develops, we learn to enjoy spending time with Him. When we learn to hear His voice and walk with Him, it even becomes fun! If you've never had that kind of connection with God, it is something that you can cultivate. It's not instant, but if you pursue it, it is possible. I challenge myself, along with you, to put this relationship in the place of the highest priority so that we will sincerely take delight in God and enjoy the pleasure that He will receive from us.

First Day in Heaven

The movie *I Can Only Imagine*, based on the song by MercyMe, is a beautiful story of redemption and the promise of heaven for those who are in a relationship with God. If you aren't familiar with the song, the writer wonders what his reaction will be to meeting Jesus for the first time in heaven.

I've also seen a post shared several times on Facebook that features a painting called *First Day in Heaven* by an Egyptian artist named Kerolos Safwat. (I don't have permission to post the picture here, but he has a Facebook page where the painting is pictured. Please check it out.)

The painting depicts a young woman who seems to have just entered heaven and is jumping into the arms of Jesus with a look of complete joy on her face. If you are a follower of Jesus, perhaps you've pictured that moment for yourself, when you'll finally see the One you have loved for such a long time.

It made me think about that first meeting for me and what it will be like, just like the questions that the song explores. Then I tried to think of an earthly situation that would be similar and came up with this scenario.

Suppose you write to a famous person. Perhaps it's a fan letter to a singer or actor. Maybe it's a letter to a writer or lecturer whose work you admire. It could even be a person who is not a household name but is well-known in your field of work. You write to this person to let him know how much you appreciate his contributions to his area of expertise. You don't expect an answer from him, because you know he is far too busy with his career to notice you. You just want to let him know his actions have touched you in some way and made your life better, or more enjoyable, or helped you to make progress in your career.

Then, to your great surprise, a reply comes in the mail. The person responds to your message and some of the ideas you expressed. Perhaps he asks for your opinion on a project that he is about to undertake. This person values your thoughts and ideas. Amazing! You eagerly write back, and soon an exchange of letters and emails begins to take place. Maybe you even have a phone conversation or two. For several years you keep up this pen-pal relationship with the person you admire.

After some time you find out the person you now think of as your "Person" is going to be in a city near you for an event, and he has asked if you could come so he could meet you. Are you kidding? Of course you will! He tells you that you are welcome to bring a friend with you, and the two of you will be his special guests.

The day finally arrives. Your friend, who is also an admirer of this person, is very excited to meet him as well. You enter the room where you will meet, and two very different interactions take place. Your Person strides toward you, arms wide open, and says, "It's about time!" as he gives you a warm hug. Your friend, however, meekly extends a hand for a handshake and says, "It's an honor to meet you." While your Person is warm and welcoming to them, your friend gets left in the background while you and your Person pick up where you left off in your last communication.

The difference is *relationship*. I've been struggling lately with being busy with Kingdom activities (as well as earthly ones) and not spending enough time cultivating my relationship with God. This Jesus, who I want to meet, needs to be more than just someone that I have knowledge of and whose work I admire. I need to be in constant communication with Him. I need to read His letters eagerly and reply to Him with my thoughts. I want to partner with Him in the projects He desires to undertake. I want to be like the girl in the painting. When my time to meet Him comes, I don't want just to say softly, "It's an honor to meet you, Sir." I want to jump into His arms with abandon, saying, "Hey! We were just talking, and now look...here you are!"

78 and 29

I recently attended a wedding shower where one of the party games was to guess the number of candies in a jar. I have been historically terrible with this activity, always underestimating the number by quite a bit. So, attempting to apply that experience to my guess this time, I estimated as usual, then added about 20 more to my guess. Then I chose a number that was not a multiple of 5, thinking that whoever filled the jar probably wanted to make it trickier. My educated guess was 78. To my amazement the bride-to-be announced that the winner, who had guessed the number exactly, was me! The prize for this feat was to take home the jar of candy.

At home I told the story to my husband, but I did not divulge the number or any hint of the amount. He walked by the jar, barely taking a glance, and said very casually, "78." My jaw dropped! Not only had I done the practically impossible by guessing the exact amount, but he had just matched my answer without even taking time to examine the jar! What in the world?!

A few days later, we visited a large flea market in search of an elusive item we needed for a project. We had walked through all the buildings by the upper parking lot. Then we walked down a set of concrete stairs to the rest of the buildings. After a fruitless search of those vendors, we headed back to our van by way of those same concrete steps. We walked side by side up the steps with no conversation, but when we reached the top, we both spontaneously looked at each other and said, "29!" That was the number of steps on the staircase. We had both been mentally counting, for whatever reason, and decided at the same moment to make that big announcement.

What is my point? People say that when a couple has been married for a long time, they can finish each other's sentences. How does that happen? It's not because they once stood at an altar and made promises to each other. It's because they have talked together day after day, year after year. They have seen each other react to many situations. They have listened to each other tell the same stories to other people over and over. A commitment of many years together makes it possible for two to become one. The knowing is in the life together, not in the vows.

I believe it's like that in our relationship with God. We begin to talk the way He talks, know His heart, and think as He thinks, only as a result of spending time with Him. It doesn't happen automatically the day we go to an altar and repeat a prayer, vowing to follow Him. The knowing is in the life together, not in the vows.

In and Amen

Sometimes, when I'm not in serious Bible study, I just flip through the pages of my Bible, looking at words or verses I have highlighted or underlined in the past. I was doing that the other night when I thought about the fact that the Old and New Testament are one continuous story of the love of God and His plan to reach us and bring us into a relationship with Himself.

As I thought more along those lines, I considered beginnings and endings. I knew the first word of **Genesis 1:1** was "In," but I wasn't sure about the last word of Revelation. I looked up **Revelation 22:21** and confirmed that it was "Amen!"

I am quite aware that there are 66 books in the Bible and that the book of Timothy says, **"All Scripture is given by inspiration of God, and *is* profitable for doctrine, for reproof, for correction, for instruction in righteousness..."** (**2 Timothy 3:16**). I am in no way saying that we shouldn't read and learn from every word, but really, the first word and the last word sum up the whole theme of the Bible.

Throughout the Old Testament, God was trying to establish a relationship with His people. He wanted to be *IN* their midst, desired for them to live *IN* His ways and walk according to His laws. That system of the law showed men how impossible it was to live in holiness in their own strength, how much they needed a Savior. The New Testament reveals the sacrifice of Jesus, which made it possible for us to be *IN* Him and He *IN* us. His Holy Spirit lives and works *IN* us. From "*IN* the beginning" to the Holy Spirit *IN* us, that was the plan of God.

"Amen" means "so be it." The book of Corinthians says, **"For all the promises of God in Him are Yes, and in Him Amen, to the glory of God through us"** (**2 Corinthians 1:20**). That final Amen in Revelations goes like this: **"The grace of our Lord Jesus Christ be with you all. Amen"** (**Revelation 22:21**).

The grace that John is referring to there is that same grace that causes us to be IN Him. The book of Acts says, **"...for in Him we live and move and have our being..."** (**Acts 17:28**). The most important decision we will ever make is choosing to be in Him. Everything else in our lives flows from our relationship with Jesus. What about it? Are you *IN*? Amen!

He Knows My Name

I have been doing some purging of my belongings, trying to simplify my life a little. Though I plan to live to a very ripe old age, I don't want to leave too much clutter for my children to sort through when I'm gone.

One thing I ran across in my sorting was a yearbook from a school where I taught about 12 years ago. It's the only yearbook I have from any of the schools where I have worked. In deciding whether to keep it, I looked back through the pages to see which students I remembered. I am a resource room teacher, so I didn't have a classroom of students. Instead, I worked with small groups of every grade level throughout the day. There were checkmarks beside the pictures of the students with whom I had worked.

As I looked at those faces from over a decade ago, I smiled at some as I remembered a specific interaction with them or a trait they had that I recalled. One of them was a little boy who fell asleep so much at school that I had to start having him sit on the floor to work with me so he wouldn't put his head down on the desk and start snoring! Wondering where life had taken some of these kiddos, I did what everyone does these days when they are looking for someone: I typed their names into the search bar on Facebook!

When I knew these students, they were in kindergarten through fifth grade, so 12 years for them meant their entire school career and the beginning of their adult lives. Many of their profiles showed evidence of continuing their education after high school, starting careers, developing relationships, and, in at least one case, having a child.

What was interesting about my search for them was that some were easy to find. Those students had names that were unique enough that there weren't pages and pages of people with the same name. Many had their city listed, and it was in the same area of the school where I had known them. Of course, some of them may not even be Facebook users. Others, however, got lost in the ordinariness of their names, and without a context of location, I could not pinpoint which person with that name was my former student.

Have you ever googled your name? In my case there is a famous South African rugby player named Jan Ellis and another Jan Ellis who is an actor. Ironically, there are many women with the name Jan Ellis who are also teachers. Others are writers, lawyers, and financial planners. There is even a dessert called Jan Ellis Pudding!

With all those folks coming up as search results for Jan Ellis, someone who was looking for me might have a difficult time determining just which one was me, but God knows precisely which Jan Ellis I am. I don't get lost in His mind in the multitude of others who share my name. He knows me intimately in a way nobody else can.

The book of Luke says, **"But the very hairs of your head are all numbered. Do not fear therefore; you are of more value than many sparrows" (Luke 12:7).** How about that? He knows the number of every color-treated strand of hair on my head!

The book of Revelation says, **"'He who has an ear, let him hear what the Spirit says to the churches. To him who overcomes I will give some of the hidden manna to eat. And I will give him a white stone, and on the stone a new name written which no one knows except him who receives it'" (Revelation 2:17).**

Bible scholars don't all agree about the meaning of this passage, but many of them list several cultural uses of a white stone. One was the use of a white stone by the member of a jury to cast a vote for acquittal—a judgment of being innocent of the charges. Another use of the stone was as a ticket for admission to a festival. Both of those explanations have some deep spiritual significance, but it's that new name that is most interesting to me. There are also differing opinions about the nature of that name. I think that God has a unique, identifying name for us that represents our transformation and the events of our journey in Him. We will instantly identify with and understand that name and all that it means. No one else will "know" the way that we "know" all that the name encompasses, because they didn't live our story.

At any rate, for now, I do know that He knows me better than I know myself. He knows where I was then, where I am now, and what my future holds. Though I'm just one in a vast number of all the human beings who have ever lived on this earth, he still knows me and values me as if I am the only person on this earth, and He places that same love and value on you. Don't underestimate our extraordinary God's capacity to differentiate between you and the billions of others who are in His heart. He knows your name!

Who Gets Your Attention?
(Bella at 20 months)

Have you ever realized, just as you were saying something, that the words you were using had a double meaning? Sometimes I will say something quite ordinary that turns out to be one of those phrases about which I can say, "That'll preach!"

I had a moment such as that one weekend. Our darling Bella, who gets to be the subject of so much of my writing, is a busy toddler. She is so busy exploring the world that we don't get much cuddle time with her anymore. The rarity of her hugs and kisses makes them precious, especially when she gives them without request.

She was busy that Saturday morning, playing with her toys, checking out the pantry, looking out the window, and babbling on about something, when my husband asked her for a hug. She stopped what she was doing, reached up for him, and wrapped her little arms around his neck. "Aww, thank you!" he said and put her back down on the floor. Emboldened by his success, I asked for a hug, too, but little miss said, "No," in her tiny little voice and toddled off into the kitchen.

"Wait a minute!" I said. "I feed you, and I change your diapers, and *he* gets the hug?" Before the last word left my mouth, the Holy Spirit had already stopped me on that thought. *How many of your needs has God supplied, and where do you center your time and attention?*

I had to admit that I give more of my focus to the things of the world, the petty details of daily life, and my amusement than I invest in the things of God. I find myself preferring to be entertained by things that have no value than to spend time in the presence of my Father. The enemy's most effective tool in the life of a Christian is not to draw us into gross immorality. He merely needs to distract us from our life in the Kingdom, make us prayerless and thus powerless. When we stop pursuing Jesus, it's a slow drawing away that can leave us in a place we never would have chosen to go willingly, though it's those daily choices that we "will" that take us there.

So today I vow to set my affection and attention where it belongs.

"Set your mind on things above, not on things on the earth" (Colossians 3:2).

That's where I'll start—by remembering where I belong and who deserves my focus. I won't do it perfectly, but I won't use that as an excuse to stop trying.

Power Source

Every night, before I go to bed, I plug my cell phone into the charger and put it on my nightstand. As a woman of the 21st century, my phone has become my camera, my computer, my calculator, my library, and, most importantly, my alarm clock. I rely on that phone by the bed to make sure I get up on time in the morning so I can prepare to head out to my job at a local elementary school.

After I am up and moving in the morning, sometimes I'll stop to take a quick look at the weather or my email. One morning last week, when I looked down at the screen, I was surprised to find that the power percentage on the phone was in the single-digit numbers. How could this be? I'd had it plugged in all night!

After doing a little investigating, I found that although I had the phone connected to the charger, I had not plugged the charger into the power strip on the floor beside the bed. I have no clue how or when the plug became dislodged from the outlet, but it certainly explained why my phone was nearly dead first thing in the morning.

My life is a little like that cell phone sometimes. I'll plug it into things that I think are beneficial to me, like church activities or listening to praise music in the background when I'm doing something around the house, and expect those things to give me spiritual nourishment. Those things *can* be beneficial for our spirits, but if we're just going through religious motions and we don't have our hearts truly focused on God, then those activities are not "plugged in" to the real source of power.

What can this look like in our lives? We can continue to struggle with the same life-controlling issues for a very long time while, on the outside, looking like we are trying to connect with God. We can attend church but not engage with the Word of God the pastor is preaching. We can occupy ourselves during the sermon by making a grocery list or checking out social media on our phones instead of taking sermon notes. We stay until the service is over because it wouldn't look right to slip out early, not because we are seeking Him. We can even come to the altar and ask for someone to agree with us in prayer, addressing the circumstances in our lives. What's wrong with this picture? We haven't plugged our cord into the power source. We're just waving a charger around to show people that we are trying to do what's right.

In a world that seems to be getting further and further from God, shouldn't we, as His children, be connecting with Him in a way that is real and vital and life-sustaining? Religious activity will never change the heart. Going through the motions will not transform or sanctify us. A real connection with God will do all those things and more. Even those who have been "in church" for a long time can find themselves growing complacent and disconnected.

What I'm talking about here is drawing near to God. When I looked for the phrase "draw near" in the Bible, I found two very distinct ideas. I leave you with the same question I'm asking myself: Which of these Scriptures pertains to you?

"'These people draw near to Me with their mouth, And honor Me with their lips, but their heart is far from Me" (Matthew 15:8).

OR

"...let us draw near with a true heart in full assurance of faith, having our hearts sprinkled from an evil conscience and our bodies washed with pure water" (Hebrews 10:22).

Diamonds in the Dark

One morning I was sitting in church, listening to the announcements before the sermon began, and I glanced down at my hands in my lap. On my left ring finger was my thin gold wedding band, and above it was a diamond ring, which is composed of one small diamond in the center surrounded by six additional small stones—a diamond cluster. As I moved my hand just a little, the lights in the church sparkled as the gems on the ring reflected them.

Have you ever looked at a diamond when the light is dim? It's rather unremarkable. Without light to reflect, it may just as well be a piece of glass. To display its beauty, it must be in full light. Without the light it's a diamond in the dark, without any loveliness of its own.

A raw diamond often looks like just any other rock. It's not until someone recognizes the potential in that stone, seeing what it could be, that a master artisan can transform it into a sparkling piece of jewelry. It must be cut and shaped by the hand of someone who has mastered this craft. The craftsman scrutinizes the diamond to determine the orientation of its crystals. Then the gem cutter must consider any flaws in the stone to decide how to cut it to remove them. Facets are cut into the gem to help it reflect as much light as possible. It is then polished to a high luster and placed in a setting that displays it in a way that emphasizes its beauty.

A diamond is a lot like a person. We may look insignificant and ordinary, but God sees us for what we are in His mind. He sees the potential for beauty in us when nobody else does. God already knows His design for us, and He is acquainted with every flaw in us. Armed with that knowledge, through the Holy Spirit, He begins the process of shaping us, removing the imperfections and designing the facets of our lives so we can reflect as much of His light as possible.

We have two responsibilities in this process. The first one is to submit to the Holy Spirit so we can let Him do His work in our lives. The second is to stay close enough to His light so we can reflect Jesus in this world. If we spend our time in the darkness, there is no light to reflect.

The ring that caused all these comparisons in my mind today is not an engagement ring. When my husband and I were engaged, neither of us had much money. An engagement ring wasn't in the plan. I was content to marry him using the wedding rings that my mother and father had worn throughout their marriage. Both of my parents had already made heaven their home years before my wedding. We engraved our initials and our wedding date beside theirs and prayed that our union would be as solid as theirs had been.

One day, about a month after our wedding, after a church service, a woman came up to me and said, "God told me to give you this," and she put this very ring in my hand, closed my fingers around it, and walked away. When I looked at it, I was astonished to find that the diamond ring's gold band was an exact match in width to the wedding band that I wore, making a perfect set.

Later that summer I distinctly remember being at my grandparent's farm, walking around in the beautiful sunshine of a country afternoon, and looking down to see the sunlight reflecting from that ring. I asked God then why He gave this to me, and I heard in my heart so clearly, "I just wanted you to know how precious you are to Me."

Each of us is a precious, unique jewel to our God. If we continue in Him, it's incredible to think about what He can create in us and how much His light can shine to others as we reflect His amazing love.

The book of Peter likens us to this precious stone. **"Coming to Him *as to* a living stone, rejected indeed by men, but chosen by God *and* precious, you also, as living stones, are being built up a spiritual house, a holy priesthood, to offer spiritual sacrifices acceptable to God through Jesus Christ" (1 Peter 2:4-5).**

Shining in the Darkness

One evening, as the daylight began to dim, my husband looked out at the shed in the backyard, where we have a solar light attached to the right of the door. He remarked that it hadn't come on yet, though other solar lights in the yard were burning. Looking out a little later, though, it had finally begun to shine. It made me curious to find out how solar lights work.

There's a solar cell that changes the sunlight into direct electrical current. That cell is the dark panel you see on the top of the light. Without getting into all the technical jargon, the short story is that there are layers of negatively-charged electrons and positively-charged spaces in the cell. When the sunlight comes through the cell, it stirs up those negatively-charged electrons and forces them into the positively-charged spaces. Then the electron stream is transferred into a direct current of electricity, which is stored in a battery until it is needed.

Later, when there is no sunlight to convert, a photoreceptor senses that it is dark, and the light turns on, supplied by the battery which has stored the power. The light will shine until the battery dies or until the photoreceptor can tell that the daylight has returned.

Why have I suddenly started writing about science instead of spirituality? As usual, God takes the mundane things in life and shows me something that I can apply to my life. We are like the solar light. Our spirits are like the solar cells soaking up the sunlight of the glory and love of God, which can push the negatives in our lives into positive new places. Then we are open to the power of the Holy Spirit, which we "store" in our hearts and shine on others when they need His light in their lives. We will have moments in our lives when we will sense that a situation is in darkness, and we'll know that it's time to release what God has given to us. Just like the solar light, we can only shine if there is power within us, so we should always be seeking to be in the beautiful light of His presence so we can stay continually filled.

In the Center

Spring is the season of graduations, and each year I attend the awards ceremony marking my elementary school's fifth-grade students' transition to middle school. As a teacher I was sitting among a large group of parents, grandparents, and other well-wishers at the last ceremony I attended. The students sat in a section of seats in front of us. Each child would stand, turn, and face the adults as they heard their name announced for an award. At one point the entire class stood and faced us as they sang a song they had practiced. As the song continued, I saw a sea of cell phones rise in front of my eyes. I was looking at the entire class of about 80 children singing in unison, but the image on each of those cellphone screens was very different. Every picture centered on a different child. No two people in that room saw that scene the same way, because they focused their attention on someone they loved.

That's how life works. All of us have our attention centered on the things that mean the most to us. We spend our time, energy, money, concentration, and affection on what we deem to be most important. As I noticed those screens across the room all focused on a specific someone, God seemed to be asking me where the attention in my life was focused. Yes, it's good and right to love people, to focus on your family members and their wellbeing, but the very center of our lives needs to be our relationship with God. Without the strength, love, and wisdom He gives us, we can't effectively love others anyway.

"But seek first the kingdom of God and His righteousness, and all these things shall be added to you" (Matthew 6:33).

How do we do this? How can we work full-time jobs, manage households, interact with people, care for children, and still be putting God first in our lives? Not many of us can be the kind of person who can just lock ourselves in a room and pray and study for hours on end.

When I looked up the definition of focus, it gave me a little clarity about how this is even possible. One of the meanings is: a point at which rays (as of light, heat, or sound) converge or from which they diverge or appear to diverge.

To me all the different things that we juggle in life are like the rays of the sun. There is life in the *divergent* actions of our lives if they are rooted in our relationship with God. Those actions bless others like the rays of the sun provide heat and light for the earth. Likewise, if we do those things in love and obedience to the various calls that are on our lives, we do them as unto the Lord, and those acts *converge* back to Him as acts of praise. God calls us first to be His children, but within that call are other roles, such as being a godly spouse or parent. There are calls to various types of ministry, where we use the gifts that God has placed in us to serve others in our lives and our churches. Yes, Bible study and prayer are necessary to develop that intimacy with God and learn to hear and recognize His voice. However, we focus and keep Him in the center by the daily living of our lives, keeping Him in mind as we go through our daily routine.

"For of Him and through Him and to Him are all things, to whom be glory forever. Amen" (Romans 11:36). It's all about Him anyway. He is the center. Where is your focus?

Focus on the Cross

At my last annual eye exam, I was seated at a series of different machines throughout the appointment. As I got my head into position at one such instrument, the eye doctor's assistant explained that during the test all I had to do was to "focus on the cross." Of course, that phrase immediately screamed *this week's blog post*, so I paid close attention to the mechanics of that exam.

As she changed settings on the machine, I followed her directions by focusing my eyes on a small cross glowing with a green light on the screen. As I maintained that focus, I could see a series of red lines moving in chaotic, agitated patterns in my peripheral vision. The screens changed from time to time, and the cross moved to various positions. Sometimes all the lights went off at once. When that happened there was always an after-image of the cross bathed in royal purple light, but no sign of the former red lines.

Since I was already listening to hear the spiritual lesson in this normal part of my yearly exam, understanding came quickly. No matter how frightening and angry the chaos in our lives may look at any time, we must keep our eyes on Jesus. He is the constant in an ever-shifting world that can bring confusion. Even though He never changes, we may need to shift our focus to see Him working in different ways in our lives. Though His character remains the same, sometimes His methods can be unpredictable to us, so we need to adjust our concentration to make sure we are tuned in to Him and not just to a solution for the current problem we are facing. Someday our lives on this earth will be over. We will not remember the difficulties, the turmoil, the fear, or the pain. We will see only Jesus in His royal glory.

I pray always to maintain that kind of focus on the King.

Spiritual Vertigo

One Friday morning I woke to the alarm on my cell phone. I reached over to turn it off, still flat on my back. Then the world tilted to the right, and I felt like a chicken on a rotisserie flipping over to finish the cooking process, but I hadn't moved an inch. Vertigo had given me the perception that I was moving when I was not.

I kept having that feeling intermittently over that weekend, so like anybody in this information age, I started researching it on the internet. I found that the most common reason for vertigo is something called "benign paroxysmal positional vertigo." It is caused by tiny calcium particles that are naturally present in a jelly-like substance in your ear. They move out of place and clump up in canals of your inner ear, distorting your perception of gravity and balance. Nothing foreign or infectious has entered your body. Something is just in the wrong place.

About four years ago, I was working with an adorable little blond kindergartner at school when, across my field of vision, what looked like a worm appeared. I was wearing contact lenses then, and I assumed that a tiny hair or piece of fiber from my clothing had made its way into my eye. As soon as I was free to check it out, I removed the lens and found that the "worm" was still there. After a visit to my eye doctor, I found that this was my first real experience with a "floater." Floaters are also part of something natural. The jelly-like vitreous inside the eyeball becomes more liquid, and little fibers clump up and cast shadows on the retina. Again, something that was a natural part of my body moved out of place, and this time it caused me to see something that wasn't there at all and interfered with me seeing what was directly in front of me.

So why is this important? You don't care about the minutiae of all my little medical peculiarities. It's significant because, if you listen to what God is saying in any of your little everyday circumstances, you can learn something more profound than what the surface situation may be.

You see, there are things in my life that are natural and normal and right and good. I have a husband, children, a grandchild, friends, a job, a church, hobbies, and amusements that are all things that God means for me to enjoy. I can spend time on these people and things with no condemnation whatsoever. They are the things that make up my life. Having an interest in these aspects of my life is not sinful, but prioritizing any of them over my relationship with God is missing the mark. When these things move into the wrong place, I experience spiritual vertigo: a difficulty with keeping my balance, an interference with my perspective. Little "floaters" of distraction move across my spiritual vision, obscuring the God I should be looking to above all things. I have been guilty of this so often that I should have learned this lesson well by now. Sometimes God must show you something many times before you finally understand what He is trying to say.

One home treatment during an attack of vertigo is called "visual fixation," where you pick a spot on the horizon and focus your vision there while you are moving. The floaters finally cleared up on their own, and vertigo gradually subsided. I didn't have control over either of these conditions, but I have control over my spiritual vision and balance if I submit them to God and keep my focus on the horizon He has set for me to seek.

The Bible says it this way: **"I have set the Lord always before me; Because he is at my right hand I shall not be moved" (Psalms 16:8).**

"If then you were raised with Christ, seek those things which are above, where Christ is, sitting at the right hand of God. Set your mind on things above, not on things on the earth. For you died, and your life is hidden with Christ in God" (Colossians 3:1-3).

Theme 4:
Prayer — Just Talking to Your Father

A Unique Conversation

When I think about my prayer life, I sometimes wish that I could just listen in on the prayer time of someone I admire spiritually to see how they spend their time with God, to see how to do it "right."

Then I realized that when I happen to listen in on a conversation between my husband and my son, it sounds far different than a conversation between my husband and my daughter-in-law. Because of the difference in their relationship, the time they've known each other, and their shared experiences, they communicate in different ways.

In the same way, each of us has a unique relationship with God that will express itself differently in each of us.

If you look at Biblical prayers, you can see the contrast between the eloquent prayers of David, the boldness of Elijah, the humility of Hannah, etc.

Though we need to study types, methods, and tools for prayer, the bottom line is that we just need to meet with our Father and spend time with Him. Don't hold yourself to an unrealistic standard that you imagine everyone else is achieving.

Spiritual Dehydration

Several years ago I realized that I was feeling spiritually "dry." As I meditated on the reasons, I thought it might be because I missed a church service when I had recently been out of town or because there were many situations that I'd been praying about that seemed to be at a standstill.

Though both may have been factors, the main reason was that I had let my times with God in prayer and study take a backseat to other things in my life.

As I thought about that dryness, God brought some thoughts to my mind about how I deal with dryness in other situations. If my hands are dry, I apply hand lotion. If my mouth is dry, I get a drink of water. If my gas tank runs dry, I go to the gas station and buy some gasoline. The moment I notice the need in those situations, I immediately take care of it. Why do I hesitate when I feel spiritual dryness in my life?

There is only one cure for spiritual dehydration: getting soaked in the water of the Word and the spirit of God. The book of Psalms says, **"O God, You *are* my God; Early will I seek You; My soul thirsts for You; My flesh longs for You In a dry and thirsty land Where there is no water" (Psalms 63:1).**

The Bible compares being away from God to being thirsty, but Jesus told us that he would give us living water. He said to the woman at the well, **"Whoever drinks of this water will thirst again, but whoever drinks of the water that I shall give him will never thirst. But the water that I shall give him will become in him a fountain of water springing up into everlasting life" (John 4:13-14).**

God knew that each of us would feel these times of drought, and He made provision for us. In those times, when our emotions seem to tell us that God is far away, we can know that through the Word and the Spirit which He has given to us, we can find refreshing.

It's Okay to Be Hungry

Like most of the world, I am always conscious of my weight issues, and now and then I try to do something about it. When my doctor told me to lose 20 pounds before my next check-up, I decided to set that as a goal, so I joined a Facebook support group that was discussing the same diet program that I was trying.

One day a new member posted that she was worried she wasn't going to be able to be successful because she was already so hungry on day one. One of the other members, Spencer Sloan, posted this comment to her post:

We have to realize it's okay to feel hungry. People for thousands of years felt hunger, pain, cold, and sadness, and they were fine. In our culture today, we always want to feel comfortable. Eat when hungry, pill for pain, always keep warm, etc. It's okay to be hungry.

The moment I read that comment, I felt an immediate leap in my spirit. God used Spencer's thought to teach me something rather simple yet profound. In the last few months, I had been feeling "spiritually frustrated," thinking that I should be further along in my spiritual maturity by now, closer to God, more knowledgeable in the Word, stronger in prayer, and more effective in ministry.

What I understood at that moment was that "spiritually frustrated" translated to "hungry." When Spencer said that it was okay to be hungry, I realized that it was okay to be spiritually hungry as well. When we are physically hungry, we spend time finding something to fill us up. We gather the ingredients for that meal, and we spend time putting those elements together to create something delicious and satisfying. Hunger drives us to seek what we need and to labor to put it into a form that we can consume and use, not only to soothe the pangs of that hunger but also to nourish our bodies and please our palates.

Spiritual hunger compels us to seek the presence of God and use the ingredients of prayer, Bible study, praise, worship, and gathering with other believers to satisfy that longing inside us. Not only is that initial hunger satisfied, but God gives us the spiritual nutrition that helps us to grow and have the joy that our spiritual appetite can enjoy.

Hours after we eat, physical hunger returns. After a while so does spiritual hunger. If we get spiritually "comfortable" and don't experience that hunger, we'll stop seeking all those things that God desires us to pursue.

So I am continuing the new eating plan and losing weight. Some days I am hungry, but when those hunger pains hit, I remember to go after God with all that I have within me, and I remember that it's okay to be hungry.

Ask Me Every Day

Throughout this book there are many references to my granddaughter, Bella. There is some background to this continuing saga that I want to share because I think it will be an encouragement to someone.

My son and his wife have always wanted to be parents. The desire to have a family was in each of their hearts years before they met and married. Unfortunately, there is a fertility issue, and doctors have told them that their only hope of conceiving a child is through In Vitro Fertilization (IVF). While they considered this, they also were trained and licensed as foster parents, hoping someday to adopt a child through the foster system because private adoption is far too expensive.

In April of 2015, a sweet baby girl came into their home. Though social workers knew that Josh and Brittney only wanted to foster a child that could be adopted, they persuaded them to take her. I watched them become parents as they cared for that child. Through all the typical first-year stages, they loved her and helped her grow and develop, all along taking her for visitations to her birth father, knowing that she would probably leave them one day. That sad day for all of us came in February of 2016, when she went to her father permanently.

Later in 2016, they were able to attempt IVF with the help of a sweet friend of Brittney's who was willing to go through the grueling process of being an egg donor for them. Sadly, that one expensive attempt was not successful.

On one of the early days of January 2017, Brittney wrote something on her Facebook page about the heartbreaking year of 2016 with the loss of the foster baby and the failed IVF attempt. Her faith amazes me sometimes. In the middle of all that sadness and disappointment, she was still trusting God to build their family, and she shared that hope in the same Facebook post.

The evening that I read her post, I was sitting in my recliner, just thinking about their situation. I wished that God would bless them with a child. I wasn't even really praying, just mentally hoping. Now I don't know how you hear God, because I believe He communicates with all of us uniquely, but I saw in my spirit, just like seeing giant capital letters in my mind, this message: "ASK ME EVERY DAY."

I have prayed about this situation many times, but not necessarily every day and maybe not with as much dedication and earnestness as I could have. So, when God tells you to pray about something every day, you pray about it every day!

Four days later I was sitting at the desk in my home office when Brittney sent me a Facebook message and asked me if I had time to talk. Social services had contacted them and asked them to take a newborn baby girl. They had to decide by the next day, and she wanted to discuss all the issues surrounding this child with her parents and with us before she and Josh decided what they wanted to do. Four days later!

They decided that they wanted to pursue the adoption of this precious baby, and as of January of 2018, she is, now and forever, officially an ELLIS!

I'm not telling you that if you pray for something every single day your answer will come in four days or a week or a month or a year. I *am* saying that we should not give up in prayer. **"Ask, and it shall be given you; seek, and ye shall find; knock, and it shall be opened unto you..."** (Matthew 7:7 KJV). I've read some articles that look at the meaning of this verse in the original Greek, and they suggest that a better translation of this would be: **"Keep on asking, and you will receive what you ask for. Keep on seeking, and you will find. Keep on knocking, and the door will be opened to you"** (Matthew 7:7 NLT).

I'm also very aware that my prayers were not the only ones prayed in this situation. All I know is that the Holy Spirit prompted me to pray in this way, and the result for us is a blessing in our lives every day. Being a grandmother, watching a little one grow and learn and change, is always teaching me new lessons about God and our relationship with Him. That's why so much of my writing revolves around her. I still have much to learn about faith and prayer, but I am so very thankful for the lessons I have learned since her birth.

When I originally wrote this and published it on my blog, I said that I would wait until we got Bella potty trained before I started praying for the next baby for their family. I'm happy to announce that she was successful in that undertaking, so let the prayers commence!

What do You Want?
(Bella at 18 months)

Miss Bella is 18 months old! These 18 months have been full of milestones for her: rolling over, crawling, walking, feeding herself, and so much more. The one skill that will mean the most for her future is learning the language she'll be using for the rest of her life. Bella knows many words, and she understands so much. It's incredible to me how quickly these little people figure out the world around them. Of course, she can comprehend many more words than she can say. She has a set of baby-signing videos that teach words along with the American Sign Language symbols for those words. It's so cute to hear her ask, "More?" as she does the sign when she wants more food or more of a favorite activity.

Because we adults are so excited about her learning words, and because she is so adorable saying them, we are always talking with her, trying to persuade her to say certain things. So, when we are in the backyard, I don't just let her point to the swing; I encourage her to tell me what she wants, and she can produce a decent approximation of the word. She signs the word "cracker" while saying the word to get a snack out of my pantry. I could just anticipate her needs and wants and provide them without her speaking, but that would slow her language growth and her independence. I don't want her going through life just pointing at things she wants and grunting.

I think that is one reason prayer is so important. God knows our every need, but He wants us to ask for what we desire. Jesus asked a blind man that very question in the book of Mark.

Now they came to Jericho. As He went out of Jericho with His disciples and a great multitude, blind Bartimaeus, the son of Timaeus, sat by the road begging. And when he heard that it was Jesus of Nazareth, he began to cry out and say, "Jesus, Son of David, have mercy on me!"

Then many warned him to be quiet; but he cried out all the more, "Son of David, have mercy on me!"

So Jesus stood still and commanded him to be called.

Then they called the blind man, saying to him, "Be of good cheer. Rise, He is calling you."

And throwing aside his garment, he rose and came to Jesus.

So Jesus answered and said to him, "What do you want Me to do for you?"

The blind man said to Him, "Rabboni, that I may receive my sight."

Then Jesus said to him, "Go your way; your faith has made you well." And immediately he received his sight and followed Jesus on the road. (Mark 10:46-52)

I know that Jesus knew what Bartimaeus wanted, but he made him articulate it, just as I do when Bella has a request. I think that the point of Jesus asking was to activate the man's faith. When he had asked, he was opening his spirit to the possibility of healing. Asking Jesus, who was the One who had the power to heal him, showed that he knew he had come to the right source. When Bartimaeus requested healing, it activated his faith. Faith resulted in his recovery, and that led to Bartimaeus following Jesus. When we have a relationship with Jesus, the words of our mouth, combined with His power, create new things in our lives and change situations.

I am not Bella's source; God is. While she is little, though, she is learning that her relationship with me (and her parents and other family members) is the key to getting her needs met if she will ask for what she wants. We, as children of God, need to learn that same thing, that relationship comes first and asking comes next.

"If you abide in Me, and My words abide in you, you will ask what you desire, and it shall be done for you" (John 15:7).

Abiding in Him is the very definition of relationship. If His words abide in you, you will know His character. Then what you desire will agree with what He wants for you and will be for your good. Tell Him what you want!

It Worked!
(Bella at 18 months)

A couple of months ago, it was time for a significant change in our granddaughter's life. She had finally reached the required weight to allow us to turn her car seat around so she could look out the windshield instead of the back of the van. What a milestone! It changed her view of everything around her as we travel.

On one of the first days that she was allowed this new perspective, she was in her seat as my husband was driving to pick me up from the beauty shop. As they drove along, there was a car driving slowly in front of them. Anxious to get on down the road, Bella shouted, "Move, car, we have to drive!" Just then the car moved into the left turning lane, leaving the road free for Paul to continue. He heard a tiny gasp from the backseat, glanced back in the rearview mirror, and caught a glimpse of the shock on her face when she exclaimed, "It worked!" Bella was astounded by the apparent power of her words.

I think I'm that way with prayer sometimes. I know the words to say. I know what change I want to see, but do I always expect it to work? Have there been times when answers came almost immediately and I was surprised?

The book of Luke tells the story of the seventy that Jesus sent out to minister in the cities where He was about to go. When they returned they were joyful and said to Jesus, **"Lord, even the demons are subject to us in Your name"** (Luke 10:17). I can hear a note of surprise in their report. Even they were surprised by their authority. As Christians our words carry power.

When Jesus cursed the fig tree and He passed by it the next day, Peter exclaimed, **"Rabbi, look! The fig tree which You cursed has withered away"** (Mark 11:21). Can you hear the surprise in that exclamation?

Jesus often used the phrase, "Oh, ye of little faith!" Faith expects something to happen. After all, Jesus spoke of a faith that would move mountains.

When my prayers seem to be unfruitful, I need to examine my expectations. Am I praying polite, little, rote prayers just to be sweet or dutiful, or am I boldly coming to the throne of grace (**Hebrews 4:16**).

I want to be like Bella. I want to see things from a new perspective, declare what I want to happen, and see results, but when things change I want to celebrate what God has done and not be surprised that prayer has worked in just the way Jesus told us it would.

God gave man dominion on the earth, making him God's representative here. When Adam and Eve forfeited that legal right in the Fall, Jesus bought it back for all of us. So now we have the legal right and responsibility to invite God into our situations.

My husband gave this insightful example to make this much more understandable. It's just like renting a house. The landlord owns the house, and his name is on the deed, yet because you reside in the home, he must have your consent to enter the house. When something in the house breaks or malfunctions, it is your responsibility to bring it to the attention of the owner so he can put things right. He wants to maintain the house adequately, yet he needs you to inform him of the needs and to permit him to enter your home to make repairs.

The Bible says that the earth is the Lord's and the fullness thereof. Just like a landlord, He retains ownership but gives us the stewardship of the earth. When something is wrong (and there is so much wrong here), it is our responsibility to make those needs known to the only One who has the right, power, and resources to fix them. When you think about prayer that way, it seems a lot less like a religious exercise and more like an awesome interaction between the

God of the universe and a person who He values as having authority to intervene in a situation.

And All His Benefits...
Theme 5:

Faith and Trust: Experiencing Real Peace

Believing God

Several years ago I was in a group when a couple of people stepped all over my "God-dreams!" From their point of view, they were trying to help me, but their advice on how I should run my life was based on my current natural circumstances and not based on what God had planned for my life. It was discouraging to listen to what they thought the rest of my life should be or would be like based on my past decisions and failures.

Once I was out of that atmosphere, I went back to the dreams and plans that I had been focusing on in prayer for some time. These were things that I thought were the will of God in my life as well as issues for which I had to believe in and be patient. There are things in which the Holy Spirit had to lead me to find His perfect timing, and I decided that I would rather believe God than settle for less. I chose to believe the report of the Lord!

Ultimately, no matter who speaks into your life, you must always filter what is said through God's Word, His leading, and what you believe you've heard from Him. I'm sure that Abraham and Sarah had friends who laughed at their idea that they could have a baby at their age. Joseph's brothers ridiculed the notion that he would rule over them. Goliath taunted David for attempting to come against him with a sling and some stones. The inhabitants of Jericho probably were laughing at those crazy Israelites marching around their city. BUT GOD...

My life is like a canvas with an evolving picture emerging with every day that passes. My naysayers look at the picture and see the random brushstrokes and blobs of mistakes. They examine my palette and perceive that I've let much of the paint dry up. They think that I might as well just sit back and accept that this picture will never be beautiful, and there is not one thing I can do about it.

You see, I know that I'm not the artist at all. God is the Creator of the masterpiece. Even though I wrestle the brush from His hand sometimes and make those mistakes on the canvas, He is the ultimate genius and will turn the chaos into order, and He will make something beautiful, strong, and victorious of what others see as a failed life. Often the true beauty of a work of art is not visible at the beginning, or even in the middle, but when completed the artist's true vision is finally apparent.

When You and God Don't See Eye to Eye
(Bella at almost 3)

Have you ever found one of those temporary cartoon tattoos for children in a cereal box? Bella and I found one over the weekend, and the picture showed characters from a movie she enjoys. I sat her on the kitchen counter so I could be close to the sink to get water to wet the sponge I needed to use to apply it to her arm.

First I squinted at the tiny directions written on the back of the package. Why do they have to print things so small these days? I peeled the protective film from the front of the tattoo and placed it face down on her arm, then started pressing the wet sponge against the backing to get the picture to release and attach to her arm. Her little eyes filled up with tears as she looked down at what I was doing. She saw a white rectangle of paper with the directions printed all over it instead of the picture she had imagined was going to be there. "No! No!" she cried, and she tried to pull her arm back. She did not want this at all!

"It's okay, Bella. I need to do it this way. You need to be still and trust me so that you won't mess this up. The picture will be there in a minute," I reassured her.

To her credit she stopped crying and watched me intently as I continued the process. After a few seconds, I barely pulled back one edge so that she could see that the colors were beginning to transfer to her skin. I kept applying pressure and dabbing the sponge on the paper until the entire backing was wet and the picture on the other side was complete and visible. Then I removed the paper and let her see the finished product. She beamed up at me and started talking about her favorite character.

How often do we do this very thing with God? We have a dream—a picture of something we want to see in our lives. We know exactly how it should look. It will unfold in a certain way, on our timetable, marking specific milestones along the way. Then, when life starts veering off in another direction, we panic. "God, this isn't how it's supposed to be!"

God hears us say things like this:
- "I'm supposed to be marrying this person, but now they've left me."
- "We were supposed to have children by now, but we're having fertility issues."
- "By now I should have had a promotion at work."

- "I should be further along in ministry at this point in my life."

Or any of a hundred other things that we thought should be coming to pass.

We don't see as God sees. He says, **"For My thoughts *are* not your thoughts, Nor are your ways My ways" (Isaiah 55:8).** We look upon what is happening in our lives, at what God seems to be applying to our situation, and we're disappointed, scared, hurt, and so sure that God has missed it. These things are not what we prayed for, believed for, stood for, declared, and decreed. Or are they?

"Remember the former things of old, For I am God, and there is no other; I am God, and there is none like Me, Declaring the end from the beginning, And from ancient times things that are not yet done, Saying, 'My counsel shall stand, And I will do all My pleasure...'" (Isaiah 46:9-10).

If we do as I told Bella and be still and trust Him through the process, we may find that the picture He is applying to us is far more beautiful than the one we had imagined.

We will discover the book of Ephesians to be true if we wait on Him.

"Now to Him who is able to do exceedingly abundantly above all that we ask or think, according to the power that works in us, to Him be glory in the church by Christ Jesus to all generations, forever and ever. Amen" (Ephesians 3:20-21).

Supernatural Provision

Several years ago my husband and I embarked on a commitment to tithing. Tithing is the Biblical principle of bringing God the first ten percent of your income as an act of worship and trust. It's introduced in the Old Testament and affirmed by Jesus in the New Testament. I believe it's not a money issue but a heart issue. Since we first made that commitment, we have had both times of abundance and times of lack, but through all of it, we have seen God working in our lives in a variety of ways, and they aren't all related to our bank balance.

One early November day, not long after we began this practice, I recorded in my journal a series of events that taught me just how much I can depend on God to meet my needs when I am obedient to Him. I had just had a payday, and I'd written my tithe check, paid bills, and bought groceries. Then I realized that I did not have enough money to buy gas to get through the entire work week. There was a fleeting temptation to get a bad attitude and declare that this concept of Kingdom finances—tithing and offering—was not valid, but instead, I went to God. I reminded Him that I was a tither and a giver, and I thanked Him that I could expect provision in my life.

My adult son was living with us at the time, and he always had extra money because he had no real living expenses. I could have borrowed money from him, but I didn't want him to think that I looked upon him as my source. I knew of several different sets of funds that were due to me in late November or December, but they would arrive too late to help, so I just determined in my heart to trust God and go about my business.

The very next day, we received a tax rebate check in the mail that arrived a full six weeks earlier than the IRS had told us to expect it! Not only was there enough to fill the gas tank, but we were able to pay off some short-term debts and replace our decrepit car with a newer used vehicle. Then, just a couple of days later, my husband was offered a temporary full-time job at a community college nearby that promised him six months of work.

Can't you just see God planning that lovely week, setting things in motion and anticipating my delight?

I could tell dozens of stories like that. There have been seasons where we had to trust God for even the essential things and other times when we had enough to bless others. We've had times of strict budgeting and times when we had money to enjoy. What we have never had is a time when we felt abandoned and without hope. God is a good God, and He will provide what is necessary for your life, your ministry, and your purpose.

Just Hold on to the Wheel!

In 2011 my family was in a period of major transition. Our son, Josh, left home to work in Bristol, Virginia, where he had found a job at a Christian television station. It was an answered prayer for him because he was moving closer to his girlfriend, who soon became his fiancé and later his wife. Our daughter, Nikki, was in a period of turmoil with a relationship and a housing situation. My husband's term at a temporary job had ended, and he was starting a new position at a local hospital. The board of education had eliminated my educational specialist position and had transferred me to a new job that was far from our home. I was applying for teaching positions closer to home, but the future was very uncertain.

One night in the middle of this chaos, I had a dream. I was driving an old, beat-up pickup truck and was following my husband, who was driving an SUV that we owned at the time. The roads were narrow and slippery, and I took a curve too fast. The truck went airborne! It flipped over and over in the air, headed down into a valley, but it never hit the ground. Time seemed to slow down as I was holding on to the steering wheel and praying. Despite the danger I felt calm as the truck continued its continual spiral.

That's how life is sometimes. You keep going around and around your set of problems. Every day it's the same situation hitting you over and over, like an endless tumble down a mountainside. In the natural it's challenging to keep your focus on the task at hand and maintain a calm exterior. If we can keep our focus on Jesus, we can have supernatural peace in the center of the storm. The Bible calls it the "peace that passes understanding." That's because there is so much that we don't understand and may never comprehend, but our all-knowing and loving heavenly Father is in control. Just hold on to Him and let Him do all the steering!

Trusting When You Don't Like How It Feels (Bella at 18 months)

I went to a swimming party with my daughter-in-law and my granddaughter, Bella, who was not yet a swimmer. So "swimming" for her meant being carried through the water while splashing and kicking. She likes me to hold her under her arms and pull her toward me through the water while she tries to kick her little legs. It's a different story if I try to hold her in my arms and help her to lie on her back. That is something she resists.

I shouldn't have been surprised. Like many little ones, Bella does not enjoy having her hair washed. She doesn't like the feeling of the water on the top of her head or the drops streaming down her face. I know that that little girl loves and trusts me and knows that I will not do anything to hurt her. It's not that she didn't trust me to keep her above water while she lay on her back; it's just that she didn't like the way it felt.

Then God reminded me that I am the same way. I trust God. My head and heart both know that God will not do anything to harm me and that I can rest safely in His arms. Sometimes, though, I just don't like the way that feels. There are times when He is bringing me through a season in my life when the water isn't comfortable. I know

He is holding me, and I don't have any fear; I just don't like the way I feel.

During those times He is teaching me and trying to develop things in me that aren't easy to experience. Sometimes there is pain. Often there is a period of stepping out into things that don't feel natural to me. More times than not, I must see issues in myself that I'm not ready to confront. Through all of it, though, I know that I won't be dropped or left to sink and drown in the middle of my situation.

Someday, when Bella is a much bigger girl and has learned to float and swim and dive, she'll read this story and wonder what the big deal was. She'll ask herself why she ever had a problem with having her head wet. She'll learn to get past those feelings and enjoy the freedom of moving through the water on her own, just as I can learn the freedom of letting God have His way in my life.

I know we are not supposed to be moved by what we feel, but that doesn't mean we won't feel. The key is that when God is holding us on the surface of the water, we must relax and let Him put us in that floating position, even when it's not comfortable. Pulling ourselves back into that upright position keeps us away from the peace that we can have in Him. The Bible says, **"...perfect love casts out fear..."** **(1 John 4:18).** We must remind ourselves that the love that is holding us is indeed perfect and learn to embrace the sensations that are not always comfortable in the natural, knowing that God does have our best interests in mind.

Don't Sweat the Details

I am an organizer. I like to sit down and plan all the little details of a project or a vacation. Maybe part of the reason for my desire for order is a need to be in control. Writing those lists of steps makes me feel ready to begin an undertaking, while just jumping into the activity seems too frightening without those boundaries written down in black and white.

A weekly Bible study group that met at our house was doing a study on prayer. One of the aspects we discussed was having "childlike faith." I began to think about what childlike faith looks like in real life.

When I was a child, our family was fortunate enough to take many trips, most of them in an RV to various state and national parks. Some trips were as simple as a weekend in a campground just an hour away from the house. Others were as elaborate as a two-week vacation to the American West. Either way, my parents took full responsibility for planning and preparing.

Mom and Dad would tell us that we were going somewhere on a specific date, and then my sister and I just went about our everyday childhood lives until the departure date, and then we'd jump in the back seat of the car and just go. I don't recall ever asking my parents if they had a map of the route (pre-GPS), if they had cashed a check for expenses (pre-ATM), or if they had packed enough clothes for me to wear. I didn't worry about the logistics of dealing with four people and a dog and all their needs. I didn't fret about the itinerary or the car or RV maintenance or tickets to any attractions we'd visit. I was just a passenger in a vehicle that would ultimately take me to my desired destination. I believed the promise of my parents, and I just trusted that everything would go well.

How many times in my own life have I worried and wondered about how God would take care of a situation? How many times did I despair in financial need because I could not imagine how on earth He would bring the provision to me? Just because I can't see the planning He does behind the scenes does not mean He isn't using His divine strategy to bring about a result that is far superior to my earthly solutions.

If you have a problem with your vehicle and you take it to the shop, you don't go back every morning to drive it around to see if you can pinpoint the trouble. You leave it in the hands of the repairman who has the knowledge, tools, and expertise to diagnose the problem and restore the car to working condition. Taking it out of the shop's hands every day just delays the resolution and potentially could cause more damage to your vehicle.

When you take a situation to God, you must leave it with Him. If you keep taking it back to worry and strategize and fuss with it, you aren't giving Him the time to solve it, and you could be causing more harm to yourself and others when you don't trust His plan.

I don't claim to understand God's ways or His timing or His reasons for doing what He does. I only know that in those situations where I can back off and give Him complete control, He brings about the right answer at the right time I don't have to sweat the details; I can leave them in His hands.

"'For My thoughts *are* not your thoughts, Nor *are* your ways My ways,' says the Lord. 'For *as* the heavens are higher than the earth, So are My ways higher than your ways, And My thoughts than your thoughts" (Isaiah 55:8-9).

"Trust in the Lord with all your heart, And lean not on your own understanding; In all your ways acknowledge Him, And He shall direct your paths" (Proverbs 3:5-6).

Calm in the Storm

One winter night I was relaxing in my living room, listening to some praise music and just thinking about life. As I sat in my recliner in the warmth of my little house, the wind began to howl around the windows, warning of an upcoming snowstorm. Though I could hear the loud roaring of the wind, I could not feel its movement or its biting cold. My soft chair was cradling me comfortably. I realized then that life is much like that when we are in the hand of God. The traumas and problems of life will still be there, roaring around us, but we do not have to submit to being moved or chilled in our hearts by those challenges.

Theme 6:
Guidance and Direction: Walking in Confidence

He's Already There

In 2012 my husband and I moved to Abingdon, VA. We wanted to live closer to Josh and Brittney and, eventually, our grandchildren. I found a job, put our house on the market, packed everything up again for the eighteenth time, and prepared to set up a new household.

On our last Sunday in West Virginia, I asked our pastor, Stewart Farley, if I could give a brief farewell message to our church family.

God gave me the sweetest gift when I walked into the church building that morning. From the time I first considered moving away, I had thought that on my last Sunday at Rhema Christian Center, I would like to hear the song, "Let the Worshippers Arise." I hadn't heard the praise team sing that song in quite a while, and the pastor's son, Travis, who usually sang the solo part, had moved to Florida to attend college, so I did not request the song. I hadn't even told Paul what I had hoped for, yet when I came into the church that Sunday, the praise team was practicing that very song. God knew what my heart wanted, and I believe He used it as a confirmation that this move to Virginia was in His will and His plan.

That morning I shared some of the things God had taught me during my time at the church. The message of tithing there had become a foundation in my life. I had also noticed several themes through all the sermons of the past several years. I had learned:

- I have a destiny and a purpose here—now—on this earth, and God wants me to be a champion, not a victim.
- Grow up and be a producer, not a consumer. We are the saints who are to be doing the work of the ministry.
- Jesus didn't just save me *from* something; He saved me *for* something: to be useful in the Kingdom.

I shared my tithing testimony—how God made my spirit open and receptive to everything else He had for my life and made my life fertile ground. I'd learned that lesson well through a sermon series, along with a book by Pastor Farley called *The Melchisedek Key*, which I took pleasure in helping him write. I shared how, at that moment in my life, I was really "walking on water" because, in the natural, I did not have the financial means to afford the move we were about to make. We hadn't sold the house, Paul didn't have a job in Virginia, and nothing in my bank account looked like Publishers' Clearinghouse had been by my house lately with a bunch of balloons and a check, but as I had taken each step toward this change, the provision seemed to be there. It wasn't all at once, not ahead of time, not all stored up. It just presented itself step by step.

I knew God would show me His plan as I walked. He would lead us to our new church home and guide us to the other plans He had for us. I read a quote from the pastor, which said, "If failure is not a possibility, where's the victory?" At that moment I didn't even have a rental house chosen, and I honestly did not know where I'd be sleeping the night before my first day at work two weeks later, but God was already there.

That all turned out to be true, because God was in it. I found my church home at Covenant Fellowship Church in Bristol, VA, with

Pastor Michael Booker. God has used me even more there in organizational skills, in teaching, in writing, and in altar ministry. We found that elusive rental house, then eventually another, and finally, we found a home of our own with a backyard as lovely as a state park. The teaching job has changed and has become familiar and rewarding. The first grandchild has entered our lives and has taught me more than any adult ever has. God knew. God prepared. God led, and He continues to guide us.

My Proofreader

One of my great loves in life is writing. One of my other roles in this life is helping, teaching, and encouraging others. Because of these two interests, I have recently been involved in proofreading and editing the creations of other authors to help them present their ideas clearly and correctly. As I worked on such a project one night, I thought about how nice it would be if someone would proofread my life—minute by minute—to keep me from making careless errors.

Then I realized that there is a proofreader in my life: the Holy Spirit. He was given to me to be that constant Teacher and the One who corrects in gentle ways. Just as I look over an entire document to find flaws both great and small, He examines my life to find the places where I need guidance. He rewords the negative things that I may think and say about myself and writes words that line up with the Word of God. He formats the direction of my life so that everything flows together and makes sense, just as I rearrange paragraphs and insert and delete commas to make the meaning clear. The Holy Spirit was sent by God to help give us wisdom. Jesus let us know this: **"But the Helper, the Holy Spirit, whom the Father will send in My name, He will teach you all things, and bring to your remembrance all that**

I said to you. Peace I leave with you, My peace I give to you" (John 14:26-27).

When I edit something for someone, I submit it back to them so they can review the changes that I suggest. At that point it's up to them to decide if they will accept those revisions or leave their text the way it was. Like an editor the Holy Spirit speaks to my heart and mind, but it's still up to me to either listen and make those changes in my life or to stubbornly cling to the way that I want to do things.

I have created a deadline for myself to post something on my blog each Sunday night. Some weeks several events in my life inspire my writing, but other times I may struggle to keep that commitment because God seems to be silent. However, if I listen to my Editor, He speaks just at the right time.

Close Proximity
(Bella at 19 months)

It's hard to believe that just a few short months ago, my granddaughter, Bella, was just taking her first few unsteady steps. Now she's walking everywhere—and I do mean EVERYWHERE—and getting into everything. She walks so well now that she is ready to turn the walk into a run.

One day we were playing in my backyard. She thinks it is hilariously funny when I chase her and try to catch her, so we were doing a bit of that. Then I switched up the game a bit and got her to try to chase me. She thought that was fun, too, but after just a few minutes, she turned and trotted off the opposite way in the yard. I yelled to her, "Bella, you can't catch me if you aren't going the same way I'm going!"

BAM! The thought hit me immediately. That's what God is continually saying to us. We can't "catch" Him if we aren't going in the direction He is moving. Not only that, but moving away from God takes us from His protection and into places of danger.

Bella went the opposite way, and at first she was fine. She was still in a safe place in the backyard, but if she had continued to move away from me, she eventually would have wandered into areas of danger, like the woods or the street.

When we first let other things interfere with our pursuit of God, we don't notice a problem. We are still good, decent, moral people. We think we can handle this life just fine on our own. It's no big deal. The further we go in the opposite direction, the more the trajectory leads us into situations that we never thought we'd find ourselves in again.

My husband, Paul, reminded me of a similar story involving Bella's dad, our son, Josh. When he was a little fellow, just learning to ride a bike, he took a bike ride in our neighborhood. He was still using training wheels, so this was early in his skill development in this area. He had his helmet on and was riding just a little ahead of us as we circled the neighborhood. His dad told him not to get too far ahead of us so he would be safe. As he grew more confident, he peddled faster and faster and ultimately ended up hitting a rough patch of pavement. He fell off his bike, skinning up his elbows and knees. Despite the warning to stay close, he made other choices. Paul said it's like he had the helmet of salvation to keep him safe, but he forgot to remain close to his father, thus putting himself in danger.

Remember that no matter how much you think you "have it together," you cannot risk moving off the path where God is leading you. The book of Proverbs has an excellent reminder of the blessings of pursuing God. **"I love those who love me, And those who seek me diligently will find me"** (Proverbs 8:17).

What I Thought I Wanted

I only put sunscreen on my body once this past summer. Before you think me reckless and unwise, let me tell you that, though I prefer warm weather to the stark and bleak cold of winter, I don't relish extreme heat, either, and I hate sweating! The time I spent outdoors last summer was in short periods that weren't in the peak times of day for the sun to do its damage.

When I was a teenager, though, I strove to get that "healthy-looking" tan. My friends and I would lie out in the backyard on lawn chairs, slathering on a mixture of iodine and baby oil, flipping from front to back at regular intervals to fry ourselves evenly. Unfortunately, it was to no avail. My daughter says I am the whitest white woman she knows! I think she is referring to more than the hue of my skin, but, indeed, I cannot get a tan by any means. I burn, peel, and go back to the same pasty white. So I made the decision early on that, since I could not get that golden glow, I'd avoid all the burns and the sweating and the frustration by limiting my time in the sun.

Many times in life, we think we need or want something, and it doesn't happen. My dreams of looking like the girls in the teen magazines did not come to pass, but there was a huge silver lining in that frustrated wish. By avoiding the sun for the last 45 years, my skin has maintained its youth better than some other folks my age. I often surprise people who learn my age for the first time. Better than that, I seem to have dodged the skin cancer bullet as well.

What's all this got to do with spiritual things? I know there are times I asked God for things in my life that I thought would make me complete or happy or fulfilled, but He didn't answer those prayers in the way I envisioned them. In retrospect I can now see the hand of God in the way He responded to the things I thought I wanted. His plan was far greater than the limited one I had designed, and some of those requests would have eventually spelled disaster for me if they had played out according to my wishes.

It boils down to this: God has a vision for our lives and a view of our lives that is so far beyond what we can imagine that the only wise thing for us to do is to trust Him. Oh, how we want to dictate to Him how things should be. We want His stamp of approval on our plans instead of seeking Him to guide us into His.

I once heard a sermon that referenced the Scripture: **"Delight yourself also in the Lord, And He shall give you the desires of your heart" (Psalms 37:4).** We think this means that if you follow God, He'll give you all the things you want, but this pastor's take on that scripture was that if your delight is in the Lord, He'll put the desires in your heart that He wants you to have—those that will bring about His purpose in your life and in the lives of others whom you touch. He is concerned with Kingdom purpose, not with granting wishes. It's an intriguing thought. Are we willing to let His desires become our desires and quit holding on to what we think we want?

Whose Hand Are You Holding?
(Bella at 2 years)

One beautiful May afternoon, my son, Josh, and daughter-in-law, Brittney, decided to take a walk on the Virginia Creeper Trail with my granddaughter, Bella, who was two years old. As they began to walk, Brittney told Bella that she had to hold someone's hand on the trail. Bella said, "I hold Bella's hand!" and she clasped her little hands together in front of her and pranced off down the path.

While that's an adorable story that will probably be retold many times in our family, it's also a picture of how we act as the children of God sometimes. We forget that no matter how much we have matured in the faith, we are still children, and we still need our heavenly Father.

Bella's parents wanted her to hold a hand for several perfectly natural human reasons, but those reasons are the same reasons we should be holding on to the hand of God as we go through this life.

1. **Direction and guidance** — As a toddler who has not walked this trail before, Bella doesn't know which way to go or even her destination, but her mother's hand can guide her. Though we sometimes think we know all about life, we don't know the wisest path to take or even what destination God has in mind for us next. We need to rely on Him to show us the steps to take and to guide us to the places in our lives that He has prepared for us.

"The steps of a *good* man are ordered by the Lord, And He delights in his way" (Psalms 37:23).

2. **Safety and protection** — Bella doesn't have enough life experience to know all the things that could potentially harm her. Though she tells me all the time, "Don't touch the bees," she hasn't had a run-in with a snake or a farmer's barbed-wire fence strung between the trail and his field. Some things will capture her attention and imagination that she'll want to check out more closely, but the loving hands of her parents will make sure that those things that entice her are not things that are a threat to her. The Holy Spirit can prompt us, warn us, and teach us about the things of this world that have been laid as a snare to draw us away from Him.

"And the Lord will deliver me from every evil work and preserve *me* for His heavenly kingdom" (2 Timothy 4:18).

3. **Insight and teaching** — Though everything in creation is new and exciting to children, they won't always notice some of the

things that an adult will recognize. Bella's daddy can lead her to the edge of the path to see a fascinating bug or lift her to peer over a fence at a calf grazing in the field. He can tell her the names of the things that she sees and can explain what is happening. If we stay close to God, He can give us insight and revelation into the day-to-day occurrences in our lives, just like seeing parallels between the behavior of a toddler and our relationship with Him! If we are close enough to listen, there is much we can learn from a God who knows everything.

"'Call to Me, and I will answer you, and show you great and mighty things, which you do not know'" (Jeremiah 33:3).

4. **Relationship and trust** — Isn't it just the sweetest thing to have your child or grandchild reach up to take your hand? The sense that your little one wants and needs the reassurance of having you close and knowing they are putting their trust in you makes your heart swell with happiness. God is the Creator of our emotions, and I imagine that He feels them as well. It must delight His heart so much when we put our hand in His, desiring to be close to Him and expressing that we trust His wisdom to lead us on our path.

"But *it is* good for me to draw near to God; I have put my trust in the Lord God, That I may declare all Your works" (Psalms 73:28).

God has used this little story about Bella to ask me some hard questions about my walk with Him. There have been times when I have hard-headedly charged down my own path, holding my own hand, and have forgotten all that is available to me in His hands. Just because my head thinks it knows how to do this Christian life does not mean that

I can do it apart from the One who gave me that life in the first place. You cannot do it by yourself, either. Don't forget to reach up for His hand.

Can You Hear Me Now?

I saw the Christian movie *Overcomer* with a group of friends from my church. Afterward, we met to discuss our thoughts about the film. Without giving away the plot, one of the main characters was a girl who was a cross-country runner. In a crucial race, the judges allowed the runners to use earbuds as they ran. She listened to some pre-recorded coaching as she ran the course. As she ran she received encouragement, direction, affirmation, and strategies to help her run the best race she possibly could.

I remarked to the group that I wish that I could hear the Holy Spirit that directly and clearly as I try to run this race of life. Wouldn't it be wonderful if, in every situation of your life, you could hear the audible voice of God guiding you? Of course, that kind of constant, tangible guidance wouldn't take much faith, and it's not the way that God chooses to direct most people. Yet we desperately need His influence along the way.

Yet, at any point in the movie race, the runner could have chosen to switch off the device and run the race her way. I think that's sometimes what I do. God uses all kinds of things to speak to us. His main avenue to get the message across is His Word, but how often do we let other things distract us and neglect reading the remarkable love story He has given us in the Bible? God uses the words of our brothers and sisters in Christ, but do we discredit their loving correction because it's just coming from another human being? If you've read much of my writing, you'll know that He uses simple, everyday occurrences to teach lessons, if I'm listening. He'll do that for you as well.

I guess I'm saying that if we don't already make use of the ways God has already used to communicate to us, why should He give us more? Sometimes I haven't obeyed the last direction I heard from Him, so He can't trust me with another yet. We must walk in the direction of what we have already received to have the next steps outlined for us.

"'...blessed *are* those who hear the word of God and keep it!'" (Luke 11:28).

Talking to God at the Gas Pump

When my son was first preparing to move to Virginia, several things began to fall in place for him all at once. I was driving home from work one day, praying and thanking God for good news for Josh.

I stopped to get gasoline, and I was standing at the pump, still praying, when God said, "I'm about to open the floodgates on your family." Then He asked, "What happens to people who are in the path of a flood?"

I answered, "The water sweeps them away, and they drown unless they anchor themselves to something."

"Exactly!" He said. I asked Him what this meant, and He just said, "Walk it out..."

It's been ten years since I had that gas pump conversation. The floodgates have indeed opened on our family. We have had a host of significant changes in our lives. Some of these changes have been easy and joyful; others have been difficult and challenging. That floodgate has allowed blessings of all kinds to sweep through our lives. We remained anchored to the God who spoke all of it into existence in the first place. We could have allowed the stress of all the upheaval damage our relationships if we had let our focus be on anything but God. God prepared me for what was about to happen, even though I didn't see it all at once. I walked with Him, and it unfolded, and it continues to unfold as I trust in His guidance and direction.

Theme 7:

Spiritual Maturity — Growing into Your Purpose

Message in a Bowl of Grapes

(This was one of the first times that God began teaching me lessons through an ordinary occurrence in my life.)

My grandmother was an educated woman, a teacher, a world traveler, but she was also a farmer's wife.

She planted and tended gardens, made most meals and desserts from scratch, and found ways to make use of everything at her disposal to care for her family. I always loved her homemade grape juice, and as an adult, when a friend offered to give me an abundance of grapes from her vines, I called my grandmother and got directions for making grape juice and grape jam.

Since then I've done that process several times. Once, when I had just moved into a new rental house, I was told by a neighbor that the grapes from the vines growing on the fence around that house were delicious, so I planned to make some juice from them when they ripened. Six months later they were ready to be harvested. So I took a large metal bowl outside and plucked grapes until the bowl was full.

Once inside I put the bowl of grapes into the sink and began to run water over them until it reached the rim of the container. Almost immediately, things began rising to the surface of the water—dead leaves, dried-up grapes, pieces of stems—and just as quickly, the Lord started speaking to me about some things in my life.

He said, "This bowl is your body, and the contents of the bowl are the things in your spirit, your mind, your will, and your emotions. The water is like my Word. As it pours over you, all dead and useless things in your life begin rising to the top to be skimmed off and discarded." I thought about that for a moment while I did just that, removing and throwing away the waste. At that point I didn't realize all the things that God was going to minister to me in the simple process of making juice.

I put my hand into the bowl of grapes and stirred them around, as I do each time I go through this process. More debris began rising to the surface of the water, and then God spoke to my spirit again. I realized this was not just a series of random thoughts of my own but that God had something to say to me.

"Your hand stirring the water is like My Hand, in the person of the Holy Spirit, stirring you up inside. After the initial washing by the Word in salvation, My Spirit continues to move inside you, always bringing issues to the surface for you to eliminate to help prepare you to produce something useful and beneficial, just as you prepared the grapes to make juice."

I put the grapes in a large pot on the stove, covered them with fresh water, and turned the heat to high. I watched the grapes as the heat began to cause them to split and release their juices into the water.

God said, "This is like all the circumstances that 'turn up the heat' in your life. When you stay in the water of the Word, in the middle of difficult circumstances, you begin releasing all the good things in your spirit. You begin to be productive and useful in the Kingdom, even though the process might be painful and you might feel as if your spirit itself is tearing." Then He asked me, "What would happen if the grapes were exposed to heat but were not in the water?"

I said, "They would be burned and ruined."

"Exactly!" He said. "When my people try to walk through heated circumstances without staying in My Word, they will 'burn out' and lose their productivity."

Now excited by all the understanding I was gaining, I watched as the grapes began to boil. Instead of the ugliness of the splitting skins of the grapes, I soon saw beautiful purple foam at the top of the pot and smelled the pleasant fragrance of Concord grapes.

"Let me guess, Lord. The foam is purple, the color of royalty, and that shows that Your Majesty is covering all the things in my spirit as I start releasing what you want me to produce in Your Body, and my praise is a fragrant sacrifice to You."

"You're getting this," He said. Then I noticed that the boiling of the water had caused the purple foam to rise to the top of the pan, threatening to boil over.

God said, "Did you notice that, though you only filled the pot one-third of the way full of water, it has now risen to the top? That's a sign that when I get involved, there is abundance; there is more than enough! I am doing so much in your life that it begins to spill over into the lives of others."

I got so excited by what God was showing me that I began to write all this down as the grapes boiled for the required twenty minutes. On the inside I was shouting, but as my family members observed me that day, they only saw me going through the steps of making juice.

Finally, the boiling period was over, and I began the final steps. I put ladles of the grapes and water through a strainer, allowed the finished juice to drain into a bowl, and discarded the skins and pulp of the grapes.

God said, "I design many processes in your life to teach you. You will understand the benefit of some lessons right away, while others you will question. The purpose of every lesson is to continually purify what is in your spirit to make the product of your life pure and holy, useful to the Body, and nourishing to others."

As I finished writing, the grape juice concentrate sat on my counter. Later I mixed it with sugar and water and served it to my family. Some I froze for use later, but whenever I drank it from then on, it reminded me that God can use the simplest things to teach us, and if we are listening, we can hear from Him anytime, anywhere, and in any circumstance.

Spiritual Vision

Pastor Michael talked to our congregation once about having a family vision. He was speaking about a mission, a purpose, a set of goals. As I was meditating about the word "vision," I thought about the parallels between natural vision and spiritual vision.

1. **Open your eyes.**

"And Elisha prayed, and said, 'Lord, I pray, open his eyes that he may see.' Then the Lord opened the eyes of the young man, and he saw. And behold, the mountain was full of horses and chariots of fire all around Elisha" (2 Kings 6:17).

Natural vision requires you to open your eyes. In the same way, spiritual vision may require you to look at your life and situation objectively. Then you can see precisely where you are now and see the gap between your "now" and what God has for your future.

2. Get correction.

"All Scripture *is* given by inspiration of God, and is profitable for doctrine, for reproof, for correction, for instruction in righteousness…" (2 Timothy 3:16).

Just as natural eyes sometimes need the correction of glasses or contact lenses, our spiritual vision needs the correction found in the Word of God. The eyes of our human understanding don't allow us to see clearly. We need the wisdom of God to bring correction to our lives.

3. Turn on the light.

"Then Jesus spoke to them again, saying, 'I am the light of the world. He who follows Me shall not walk in darkness, but have the light of life'" (John 8:12).

You can have your eyes wide open and your glasses firmly on your face, but if you are in an underground cave, you still won't be able to see. For clear spiritual vision, you need Jesus, the Light of the world, to cast light on your life so you can walk with His guidance.

4. Focus.

"Not that I have already attained, or am already perfected; but I press on, that I may lay hold of that for which Christ Jesus has also laid hold of me. Brethren, I *do* not count myself to have apprehended; but one thing I do, forgetting those things which are behind and reaching forward to those things which are ahead, I press toward the goal for the prize of the upward call of God in Christ Jesus" (Philippians 3:12-14).

If your eyes are flitting around from place to place, you won't be able to make any sense of what you see. Examining what is in front of you requires focus. The world is full of distractions in the form of other people, media, problems, and our flesh. Learning to make our relationship with Jesus our priority and our major focus brings the other things in our lives into their proper place so that our vision is clear.

No Longer a Newborn
(Bella at 1 year)

One cold January day, my son and his wife received a very welcome telephone call. A sweet baby girl had been born, and her birth mother had voluntarily terminated her parental rights. Because they were licensed foster parents, social services offered them the opportunity to take her into their home and eventually adopt her. The court date for finalizing that adoption came just a year later, and our family is so excited and happy to see her become a permanent part of our family.

That first year was a joyful time of watching this little person grow and change. When she first came home, like all babies, all she did was sleep, eat, mess her diapers, and look around a lot. Now she is a perpetual motion machine: crawling, pulling herself up by grabbing the furniture, clapping her hands, waving bye-bye, and babbling up a storm...just to mention a few of her skills. In fact, after today I'm convinced that she's a genius. Her mother called out from my kitchen for us to come and look. She was standing up at the bi-fold doors of my pantry and had figured out how to pull the knob and open the door. Now she had access to the magical, forbidden place that we always pull her out of when we have left one of the doors open.

As I thought about all this development, I compared it to our spiritual growth. The church talks about people being "born again," as we should. The problem is that many people never get past the "sleep, eat, mess their diapers, and look around" stage. They remain newborns. How sad it would have been if our little one was still in that phase almost a year after her birth. Though God loves us unconditionally, how tragic it is when His people don't grow and develop so that they can fulfill the incredible future that He imagines for them.

I have been a Christian for over 40 years, but do I act like a 40-year-old Christian? I don't know the answer to that question, because it's hard to know how that looks. I've met newly saved people whose maturity is astonishing and others who are still grabbling with basic principles of the faith years after first coming to Christ.

In looking at my own life, I have had several long periods of spiritual stagnation. Sometimes I was running from my calling. I was dabbling in all the things the world called "life." Other times I was going through times of complacency, more involved in my interests and cares than in the life of the Kingdom. Even now, when I want to become who God wants me to be, I sometimes get distracted and neglect those things that I know I need to grow.

What have we provided that has made it possible for this precious baby to make these strides? We have cared for her and met her every need. She's enjoyed our company and our interactions. We have provided her shelter and times to rest. We have introduced her to new experiences and taught her new things by modeling them for her.

In the same way, God has made provisions for our growth through His word, His Holy Spirit, and His church. We have the food of the Word, the cleansing of the blood of Jesus, and the guidance of the Holy Spirit. He provides us safety and shelter in His Church. It's also a place to experience Him and learn how to serve by watching others operate in their gifts and callings.

The difference between a newborn and us is that we have the presence of mind to know how growth works and have the decision-making ability to avail ourselves of all the resources that God has given us.

I encourage you and remind myself to continue to grow, change, learn, and become mature and productive.

Stand Fast

I was flipping through television channels one day and heard a song that talked about the American flag standing for freedom that nobody could take away. Immediately, this thought came to my mind.

"They may not be able to take it away, but we can surely give it away."

Given the assault on our rights in recent years, in the name of political correctness or national security, it is not such a far-fetched idea that the freedoms we enjoy are only ours if we hold on to them.

Thinking about our freedom as a country made me remember the liberty we have in Christ. The finished work of Jesus has purchased for us freedom from sin, from bondage, from sickness, from despair, from depression, from hopelessness, from legalism, and every attack of the enemy.

"Stand fast therefore in the liberty by which Christ has made us free, and do not be entangled again with a yoke of bondage" (Galatians 5:1). This verse means that it is possible to give up our spiritual freedom, just like it is possible to relinquish our political freedom.

The apostle Paul was dealing with the concept of being entangled with the yoke of bondage to the law. He was stressing to the Galatians that the basis of their salvation was not their adherence to Old Testament laws and rituals. We should be obedient to God because of our love for Him, not because we are trying to earn our salvation. We serve God in our lives and through our churches because we are thankful to Him and want to bring the same joy to others as He has given to us.

When my son was younger, he used to talk about getting "God-points" for attending church or doing other things that seemed godly. Are you living your life trying to earn "points," or are you resting in what Jesus has done for you? There is one way to know. Imagine yourself standing before God when He asks you why He should allow you into heaven. If your answer is anything besides pleading the blood of Jesus, then you may be relying on your works and allowing your own efforts to entangle you. They will never be enough. Just love and serve Him for the joy of it and rest in what He has done for you.

Imperfect Imitation
(Bella at 15 months)

Bella is a very busy tiny human. She crawls everywhere and recently has begun "experimenting" with walking. After about eight steps, she plops down on her well-padded, diapered rear end. She is developing in all ways as a normal, healthy baby girl.

One of those developmental milestones is learning to talk. Bella doesn't say much that you could recognize yet, but she is beginning to attach meaning to sounds. One of the things her parents are trying to get her to say is the word "up" when she wants us to pick her up. So far we get "uh" for "up," but she is trying!

Our words matter when we walk through difficult times. When we talk about the situations in our lives and the lives of others we love, we should be speaking what God says, not rehashing the nature of the problem.

After all, the book of Proverbs says, "Death and life *are* in the power of the tongue, And those who love it will eat its fruit" (Proverbs 18:21).

I often fall short in speaking as I should. It is very human to want to talk about all the details of our woes and rehearse all the issues that plague us. It's hard to put those things out of our minds and speak the things of God and the will of God as He spells it out in His Word. When we realize that is what we are doing, it's also easy to be angry at ourselves for our weakness and our unbelief.

When Bella tries to echo our words, she doesn't get it right, but every day she is getting a little closer to saying what we say. Are we angry or disappointed that her words are not the perfect imitation of ours? Of course not! We realize that learning a language is a process. We allow her the time to grow, and we delight in every attempt that she makes to communicate with us.

I think God must feel the same way. When we fail in our imitation of Christ and His ways, God still loves us. He knows that we need time to learn His Word and His ways and to be more mindful of our words. The only thing that could hurt me in Bella's acquisition of language is if she stopped talking at all, just stopped trying. When we don't get things right in our walk with God, we often just quit trying. We stop pursuing Him because we don't think we'll ever measure up. To a certain extent, that's true. We'll never get it perfectly right in this life, but God's grace accepts our imperfect imitation. The only thing that would break His heart is if we stopped trying.

Use it or Lose it

One Easter we had no company to cook for, so my husband and I decided on a steak and potatoes meal instead of a more traditional Easter feast. He had been craving some corn on the cob, so I added that to the menu. When the time came to eat, we wanted to use the little corn holders with the spikes on them that push into the cob, to protect our fingers from the heat and the messy melted butter. Unfortunately, we could not find them anywhere. We searched every cabinet, every drawer, inside any covered container, in the pantry, in the microwave cart—every place we could think to look.

We hadn't eaten corn on the cob for some time, or at least one of us would have remembered when we last used the holders and where we had put them. We muddled through the meal like true pioneers and recovered from the experience quite nicely, but this became one of those simple object lessons that God uses in my life so much. *If you don't use something, you will lose it.* That'll preach!

There are a lot of objects to manage in my household, but God has given us many things in our spiritual house as well. The Bible says, **Grace and peace be multiplied unto you through the knowledge of God, and of Jesus our Lord, According as his divine power hath given unto us all things that pertain unto life and godliness, through the knowledge of him that hath called us to glory and virtue: Whereby are given unto us exceeding great and precious promises: that by these ye might be partakers of the divine nature, having escaped the corruption that is in the world through lust. (1 Peter 1:2-4 KJV)**

Just like a physical object can be misplaced and forgotten, it is possible to disregard the things of the Spirit to the point that they are not operating in your life.

But also for this very reason, giving all diligence, add to your faith virtue, to virtue knowledge, to knowledge self-control, to self-control perseverance, to perseverance godliness, to godliness brotherly kindness, and to brotherly kindness love. For if these things are yours and abound, you will be neither barren nor unfruitful in the knowledge of our Lord Jesus Christ. For he who lacks these things is shortsighted, even to blindness, and has forgotten that he was cleansed from his old sins. (2 Peter 1:5-9).

The corn holders were mine, but they were undoubtedly not abounding, and they were unfruitful because I couldn't even locate them! If I'm not staying mindful of faith, virtue, knowledge, self-control, perseverance, godliness, brotherly kindness, and love, those things will be harder and harder to find in my life, making me ineffective as a Christian. Peter says to give all diligence to these things. I like to think of myself as organized in the things of my household, but the system broke down somewhere. At least the failure to keep all my belongings at hand has reminded me to keep the things that God has given me at the forefront of my life so that I'll use them and not lose them!

Claim What's Yours

One Friday afternoon I left work with a simple to-do list in my mind. I needed to go to the bank and cash a check, buy some gasoline, go grocery shopping, and then meet my son and his wife to pick up the baby so they could have a "date night." I completed my checklist and drove home. The weekend went as planned, with lots of baby giggles, a pleasant visit with my son and daughter-in-law, and church on Sunday.

Then came Monday and a regular workday. At the end of the day, as I left work, I called my husband, as I often do. Because he knows that I often fail to notice my gas gauge, and not knowing that I'd put $30 in the tank on Friday, he asked me to check to see how much gas I had. I laughed at his concern and told him I had plenty of gas, but when I turned the key in the van and the dashboard lit up, the needle showed the tank was on empty. That was impossible! I'd only driven about 15 miles on that $30, and once I got home on Friday, the van had not left the house. I called my husband back, and we talked about whether the gas tank could be leaking or whether someone could have siphoned gas from the tank. Regardless of the mystery of the missing gasoline, I was running on fumes, so I stopped and put a few dollars' worth of gas in the tank.

Driving home, I replayed the events of Friday afternoon in my mind, mentally retracing my steps. I knew I went to the bank, because the rest of the cash was in my purse. I remembered paying for the gas, BUT I did not remember pumping the gas. In a hurry to check off all my tasks and get my hands on that sweet baby, I'd simply paid for the gas, walked out, started the van, and gone off to the grocery store. I guess I'd had a senior moment and a blonde moment at the same time! Sheepishly, I called the gas station and asked if they had any record of someone paying for gas and then not pumping it. Of course, they did, and they were kind enough to allow me to come back and top off my gas tank.

I think many of us struggle through life like that. We find ourselves lacking something that we thought we had. We're confused as to why things in our lives seem to be missing. We review the events in our lives, wondering where we went wrong and trying to figure out why things are not working out the way we thought they would. Could it be that we have become distracted? Have we just not claimed the treasures for which Jesus has already paid the price?

What do you need today? Salvation? Paid for. Deliverance? Paid for. Provision? Paid for. Peace? Paid for. Wisdom? Paid for. The list is infinite. All that we need or will ever need has been purchased for us by Jesus. It may not always come on your terms or in your timing, but it is all there. Don't let the enemy distract you and keep you from claiming what is already yours.

Walking Without Applause
(Bella at 16 months)

Our granddaughter, who just a month ago was taking only a few tentative steps before falling on her bottom, is now toddling around everywhere. After every long trek she makes, the family will clap and cheer for her. My husband will then loudly complain (with tongue firmly in cheek) that he has been walking for years, and nobody is making a fuss over *him!*

While he's not seriously expecting any kudos for his ability to walk from point A to point B, his joke made me think about how we can sometimes be as Christians.

At the beginning of your journey with Jesus, you took lots of tentative steps as you learned and grew. Sometimes you fell, but if you were still serving God that day, that meant you stood back up and tried again. In those early days, in your mind, success may have been measured by those things that you *stopped* doing. No longer were you living in the sin that held you captive before. If you were always out partying the world's way, you found yourself celebrating in the house of God. Instead of engaging in a string of illicit relationships, you began cultivating a relationship with Jesus. If you were struggling with substance abuse, you started partaking in what the Bible calls the "new wine." Everything was different. People saw the changes in your life, and your transformation drew them to the God who transformed your life so radically. Those who were close to you encouraged you to stay strong and continue walking this new path.

Then some time passed. People become accustomed to you living a "moral" life. Those you have met while you have been on this spiritual journey have never seen the person you were before. No cheerleaders are celebrating the fact that you are still walking. What do you do then? **You do what you should have done all along.** It was never about the praise and approval of others. It was always about pleasing the God who gave you a new life in the first place.

"For this reason we also, since the day we heard it, do not cease to pray for you, and to ask that you may be filled with the knowledge of His will in all wisdom and spiritual understanding; that you may walk worthy of the Lord, fully pleasing *Him*, being fruitful in every good work and increasing in the knowledge of God…" (Colossians 1:9–10).

When nobody is noticing your growth in the Lord, keep growing. In a few months, Bella's walking will not be a new thing in our household. I doubt we will still be commenting every time she walks across a room. Instead, we'll be celebrating each new milestone she reaches. Even that will stop after a while. She will grow to be an adult, and she will set goals for herself and reach them. Some of those goals will not even be things we will ever know. She will achieve them, and she will grow and change on her own. She won't need our constant approval, and neither should we need the approval of man. We should move on from glory to glory, always desiring to please God and become the instrument in His hands that He will use to do Kingdom business.

Learning the Language
(Bella at 16 months)

Bella is learning the English language the way we all do. We talk to her all the time, and we repeat many simple daily things: eat, bath, night-night, bye-bye, hi, etc. She is beginning to repeat many words and is adding to her vocabulary almost daily.

She has Ma-Ma and Da-Da down pat. Next came Papaw. Her maternal grandfather is Pappy, and though her maternal grandmother is in heaven, she was called Nannie by her other grandchildren, so I can't claim that name. However, I have no earthly idea who I am. She has not yet settled on a name for me. We've used the name "Gran" for me, short for "Granny," which is what I called my grandmother, but evidently, that's a much harder sound to produce. We're trying Mimi and Nana and Mamaw to see what sticks, but for now I am "she who must not be named!"

She knows and loves me. She reaches for me, hugs me, gives me an occasional kiss. I have kept her in my home many times while her parents were busy with other things. We have a relationship, but she is just not too sure what to call me. I dearly love her, although she hasn't yet mastered this concept.

We learn the language of the Kingdom the same way. Words, thoughts, and principles that are part of our daily spiritual lives are repeated often by our Christian friends, our pastor, our daily Bible reading, songs we enjoy, and writers we follow. Despite that daily repetition, there are some concepts we still don't acquire easily. A common theme that you'll see in my blog posts is maintaining communication with God in prayer and Bible study. I'm not writing about that theme because I have mastered keeping it as a priority; it's repeating because I struggle so much with being consistent with it myself. Without letting myself off the hook for this discipline, I do realize that God dearly loves me, even when I am not mastering the lessons that He keeps trying to teach.

Bella can only learn what we can teach her. If she were in a situation where she had no human contact and no more exposure to language, her language learning would cease. If we live in an environment where nobody speaks the Word, where people are not sharing what God is leading them to say, where the focus of all the media we take in is the things of the world, we won't learn any more Kingdom language ourselves. We, as adult Christians, have control of what language we are learning. Let's make sure that we are getting it from the right source.

A Postscript to "Learning the Language (Bella at 21 months)

Update: Bella has christened me with the moniker of "Mamaw."

Growing up, I don't remember any of my friends having a Mamaw. Some called their grandmothers names like Granny, or Grandma, or Grandmother, or even Mimi, but Mamaw was not a name I heard. It seems to be more of a southern name, and as my husband is fond of reminding me, even though I'm a West Virginian by birth, I just barely lived south of the Mason-Dixon line. I made it by only about twelve miles. In his mind I'm not genuinely southern at all. He calls me a "Wetzelvanian" since I lived in Wetzel County, WV, not too far from the Pennsylvania state line.

A "Mamaw" in my mind is a plump farm wife with a floral dress and a white apron. I think I have the plump part down, but the rest doesn't sound like me. However, "Mamaw" goes perfectly with "Papaw," and since that's my husband, I guess we make a perfect pair.

What's the spiritual significance of this little story? I guess there isn't much on the surface. I think I just wanted to write to share with the readers who have been following our story that not only do I have a beautiful, smart, sweet blessing of a granddaughter, but she asks for me by name now. While most grandmothers think their grandchildren are miracles, the fact that she is in my life at all is a miracle.

The struggle and heartbreak of a fertility issue for my son and his wife caused the joy of this little girl to be in our lives. The circumstances of her birth mother's life, which could have led to tragic results, have unfolded to give her a wonderful life with us. Here she can be whole, happy, and normal (or as normal as she can be while surrounded by our crazy family!). It's one of those "what the enemy meant for evil, God is using for good" kind of things **(Genesis 50:20)**.

I am just overwhelmingly grateful to God for Bella's life, and I am so excited to see how He will continue to grow Josh and Brittney's little family. Things do not always work out the way that we think we would orchestrate them, but God's plan is always perfect. So, if you'll excuse me, I think I'll look for a floral dress and an apron. I've got a grandbaby to love on!

Back to the Basics

When you stop and think about it, the skill of reading the English language is very complex, yet even children as young as preschool age can begin to learn the names of the letters of the alphabet and their sounds. I recently started tutoring a young boy who is struggling with reading even though he is intelligent and has excellent math skills and mechanical ability.

As his mother observed us working together last week, she mentioned that she had worked with him on all these same skills in the past, and she wondered why he was having such difficulty mastering those skills the way her other children had. I could spout a lot of educational and psychological jargon to explain his challenges, but I believe that with the right teaching approach, he'll be able to master what he needs to be a competent reader.

In my own academic life, there were skills like that for me. In the third grade, I had a terrible time figuring out how to read an analog clock. Algebra was a nightmare for me, but as an adult, when I did some team-teaching with a math teacher, I was finally developmentally ready to understand. We're all at different places with our readiness to learn things, and there are always prerequisite skills that we need first to build new knowledge on the old.

As I was thinking about going back to square one with this little fellow, I started comparing his reading journey to my spiritual journey right now. Just as we all sometimes are, I have been through a season of time when I've been a little on the "spiritually lazy" side. As I've asked God to help me understand the roots of this hiccup in my spiritual walk, He's begun to show me that I need to go back to some basics of spiritual literacy, to study some things that I should have "mastered" and to see them in a fresh light. Just because I grew up knowing John 3:16 doesn't mean that I never need to reread it or to meditate on what it means to me and to those who I encounter in my life.

I haven't used the algebra that I learned in many years, so I doubt if I'd be very successful with it now. However, if I needed to relearn it, I could go back to the beginning and be reminded of the principles, rules, and skills I'd need to put it back into practice. God is showing me that where I am weak, I need to repeat some lessons and that there is no shame in that. The shame would be in maintaining false pride and insisting that everything was just as it should be. All of us need reminders of Kingdom principles from time to time when we are not living them out in the way that we know is best.

We all need to maintain a teachable spirit and to ask the Holy Spirit, who is our Teacher, to make "lesson plans" for us, to teach us what He knows we need to learn.

It's Time to Feed Yourself
(Bella at 2 years)

My husband and I went out to dinner one evening with our son, his wife, and our granddaughter, Bella. Throughout that busy Sunday, she hadn't eaten very much at breakfast or lunch, which sometimes happens when other things have her attention. However, when her macaroni and cheese arrived at the table, she made up for lost time!

She wielded that adult-sized fork like a pro, only occasionally dropping a piece of macaroni onto her shirt. She polished off the entire serving, plus a good-sized helping of fried apples.

The rest of us could enjoy our meals because her self-feeding skills have improved so much. We didn't have to stop and spoon-feed her. If we had tried to feed her, she would have said, "I do it!" She likes to demonstrate her growing skills and independence in the things that she can handle.

My pastor was preaching this morning using the example of the children of Israel. God delivered them from Egyptian slavery, and He planned to lead them to a land of "milk and honey," but taking that land meant that they had to fight for it under His leading and with His help. The sermon continued to explain how we can't just sit back passively and expect God to deliver His promises to us, but we have a responsibility to pick up the sword of the Spirit and fight to attain the promise of God.

The book of Ephesians mentions putting on the whole armor of God. The only people who have historically needed armor are those who are soldiers—those who fight. These verses tell us: **"Stand therefore, having girded your waist with truth, having put on the breastplate of righteousness, and having shod your feet with the preparation of the gospel of peace; above all, taking the shield of faith with which you will be able to quench all the fiery darts of the wicked one. And take the helmet of salvation, and the sword of the Spirit, which is the word of God..." (Ephesians 6:14-17).**

What I have learned is that you can't take up the sword of the Spirit if you don't know the Word, and you won't know the Word unless you pick up the Word, and you won't pick up the Word if you don't make it a priority in your life. Even if you go to church every Sunday of your life, the little bit of God's Word that you hear through your pastor is not enough to sustain you. Even little Bella understands that she has the ability, the right, and the joy of feeding herself. How much more important is it for us to feed on the Scriptures for ourselves? What we hear at church is not enough.

"But, Jan, I just don't understand the Bible when I try to read it. I get so confused." Newsflash! I don't understand everything in the Bible, either, but that doesn't mean that I can understand nothing. There are all sorts of resources and people who will help you learn the Word. There are online resources, videos, Bible study books, small groups at your church, mentors, and many versions of the Bible that aid in breaking down Scripture to help your understanding. Besides, we have the best teacher of the Word—the Holy Spirit—if we will listen to His voice and ask for His help.

My husband and I have recently discovered an online Bible study that we have embarked on together. It goes back to the very basics of doctrine, but it's helping us to strengthen the knowledge and foundations of why we believe what we believe.

Wherever you are in your relationship with God, you need His Word. I encourage you to find the tools you need to feed yourself. You can't fight with a weapon you don't hold.

Theme 8:

Ministry — Walking out Your Destiny

Fire

Several years ago our church hosted a youth conference. The unofficial theme song of that conference had lyrics that continued to come up in my heart even days after the meeting had ended. They talked about having a fire inside that couldn't be contained or controlled.

As those words kept repeating in my spirit, I began to meditate on those lyrics. If the fire of God is the Holy Spirit inside of us and it's a fire that we can't contain and can't control, what does that mean to us?

To me a fire that I can't contain is a fire that spreads outside of its original boundaries. The Holy Spirit comes to dwell in us, but the intention was never for Him to be locked away inside of us just to give us "spiritual goosebumps" or even just to work within us to enrich our relationship with God. He was given to us so we would have the power to be witnesses of the good news of the Gospel (**Acts 1:8**). The first thing that happened when the group in the upper room received the Holy Spirit was that the disciples preached the gospel, and there were about 3,000 salvations. They sure weren't bottling Him up!

If it's a fire that I can't control, it means that the flame has more power and authority than I have. Instead of treating the Holy Spirit as a spiritual thrill ride, He becomes a guide and an authority in my life. His counsel and power guide my actions. I must make a choice to submit to His control and to be led by Him so I can be significant in the Kingdom.

Just as natural fire can destroy, the Holy Spirit's fire can burn things out of your life that are harmful to you. In the Old Testament, when the three Hebrew children were in the fiery furnace, the only things that burned from them were the things that had them bound. If our desire is for our friends and loved ones to walk free from the things that are controlling them, then we need to let the fire of the Spirit of God out of the boundary of our own lives and let Him control our actions. Then, and only then, will we be walking in our full purpose in Him.

What's Stopping You?

Once, I was in a museum and had stopped to sit on a bench to rest. A young mother was there, holding a child in her arms as he slept. She initiated a conversation, and we chatted casually about what we were doing in that town and from where we had traveled. She shared with me that her sleeping six-year-old had woken up that morning with a fever and a cough. She was waiting there with him while her husband and daughter were looking at the exhibits.

I thought about asking her if I could pray for her son, but I didn't open my mouth. I prayed for him silently as we sat there, but I didn't have the boldness even to let her know what I was doing.

Later I thought about that incident and wondered why we are so often timid about reaching out to people. After all, there were only three possible outcomes that could have happened if I had asked.

1. She could have been a believer who would have thought it a blessing to find someone like-minded who would agree with her in prayer.
2. She could have been a non-believer who would have been touched by a stranger caring enough to pray for the healing of her child. That could have led to more conversation that could have drawn her to the Lord.
3. She could have been uncomfortable with my offer, whether she was a believer or not, and could have declined or walked away or gotten angry or had some other unfavorable reaction.

The first two outcomes would have been positive, and where I come from, a two out of three chance is not too bad! I would never see this lady again. At that moment, why was I concerned about what she thought about me? Why was that more important than offering her son healing in the name of Jesus?

Lord, please help me to listen to the prompting of your Holy Spirit and open my mouth with confidence, blessing people, and leading them to you.

Today is Your Day

Back in my day...

Have you ever heard someone use those words? I even saw an ad today that was talking about grandparents, and it used the phrase "in their day." When is my day? Has my day passed if I'm over 30? Heaven forbid!

When I was a teenager, I thought of someone in their 40s or 50s as old. Now that I've passed my 60th birthday, my opinion on age has changed considerably! I guess my attitude began changing when I was approaching 30 and feeling a little sad that my twenties were ending. My husband said something profound one day that changed my perspective on aging. He said, "You act like you're sorry you lived this long." I realized that getting older just meant that I was a survivor; it was a victory, not a defeat.

I don't feel old, and I don't feel as if my time has passed or that it's time just to sit back and relax. I'm just now really learning my whole purpose in this life. If God lets me live to be 100, I'll still be finding ways to serve. My roles and responsibilities may change with time and with age, but each day of my senior years is just as important to God as the days He gave me in my youth.

Our church sponsors youth conferences and has a dynamic youth ministry. I am not diminishing the importance of what God wants to do through teenagers in the Kingdom. We need to pour into our kids the wisdom of God, the strength and power of the Holy Spirit, and the dependence on Jesus that they will need to fulfill their purpose. My prayer is that they will be established and strong and will avoid some of the pitfalls of the world that the enemy will try to use to derail their destiny. I just don't want you to think that you are finished if those days are in your rear-view mirror.

If "our day" is only our youth, what is the purpose of the rest of our lives? The Bible shows us that God had a purpose for people of all ages, not just the young. For every story of a young David or Samuel, there's also a story of an aged Abraham or the elderly prophetess Anna at the temple as she saw the infant Jesus. Age means nothing to an eternal God. He can use us from childhood to old age. Every day is "our day" if we are walking with the guidance of His Holy Spirit.

Throwing Rocks
(Bella at 1 year)

Bella has always had a thick head of hair. By the time she was only about six months old, she had enough length to make a tiny ponytail. She has lots of hair, but it is soft and fine. Because of that, those little hair elastics slip out of her hair very easily. One day, when she was about a year old, my husband found one of her hair elastics on the floor and tossed it to me where I was sitting on the couch. I missed the toss, and it went back down on the area rug.

Paul and I both got down on our knees and started rubbing our hands back and forth over the printed rug, trying to find the missing band. Suddenly, we looked up and saw that Bella was right there beside us on her hands and knees, running her little hands over and over the rug as well. She had no idea what we were doing, but she was right there to help!

Later Paul said that it reminded him of a scene in an old movie called *Tobacco Road*. The main character is throwing rocks at a car that is pulling away from his house. His wife comes out of the door, sees what he is doing, and immediately starts picking up rocks and throwing them in the same direction. After the car is gone, she asks him why they were throwing rocks. Even without knowing the purpose, she was fully committed to helping her man.

There are many times when you may not fully understand what your pastor or other leadership folks in your church are doing. Someone may ask you to use your talents and time to help with a program or event. If you trust the integrity of the leadership, shouldn't you jump in with both feet and labor along with them to bring the vision of your church to pass?

Stretch Out Your Hand!

There are many times in our spiritual journeys when we experience profound times in the presence of God. It may be a dynamic worship service or a time of revival. A long-awaited answer to prayer may have us on a spiritual high. God may have used someone to minister to you with a timely word that made you feel precious and valued by Him. We must use those times when we have moved to a new level in the Holy Spirit to devote ourselves even more to the plans and purposes of God.

Pastor Michael once preached about resisting the urge to dig up our past failures or to dwell on our past successes. Even though I embraced that message and felt that I'd moved past those things, I was still struggling with what I saw as my current limitations. We all tend to compare ourselves to others, to see our areas of weakness, and to doubt our abilities and our gifts.

There's a story in **Luke 6:6-10** about a man who had a withered hand. I can imagine that, just as we try to hide our flaws from the public now, this man probably kept this hand tucked out of sight in the folds of his clothing. After all, it was withered, useless, a symbol to him of his inability to be productive.

Jesus said two things to this man. "Arise and stand here." And then, "Stretch out your hand." The man was about to receive his healing, but there were actions required of him in the process—actions of obedience that brought the blessing.

He stretched out his hand toward Jesus, and as he did his hand was restored as whole as the other one. I believe the healing happened AS he was stretching out his hand. If he had kept it hidden away, it would have remained as it was.

In the same way, if you have been holding back in some area of your relationship with God, such as tithing or prayer or being afraid to step out and join in a ministry at your church, God can give you strength in that area if you make the first move. That step of faith allows God to make you productive. He placed gifts and abilities within you, and even though you may not be able to see the end from the beginning, all you are responsible for doing is making yourself available and letting God bring wholeness to what you thought was inadequate. Stretch out your hand!

Imperfect Gifts

I am the world's worst at wrapping gifts. I just don't seem to have either the visual or fine motor skills to get that paper on the box neatly and evenly. I seldom even bother to add bows or ribbons, because it's sort of like putting lipstick on a pig. Yet never once have I had someone reject a package from me because of its amateur wrapping job. On Christmas morning, when my son, his wife, and our granddaughter come to the house, I doubt very seriously if anyone will mention my gift-wrapping skills (or lack thereof). We will enjoy our time together, and what is inside those clumsily adorned boxes will bring smiles to the faces of my family.

My friend, Natalie, makes the most beautiful and delicious cupcakes. They are the kind of baking creation you look at and say, "That's almost too pretty to eat." Mine...not so much. I don't have the equipment or expertise to do pretty things with the frosting, so it gets slathered on with a table knife, and that's about it. However, my banana cake with cream cheese frosting tastes delicious, even if it's not as easy on the eyes.

Did you ever watch one of those talent competitions when a very unlikely looking "star" comes on stage? The judges just sort of smirk and roll their eyes as this person takes his place and nervously raises a microphone. Then that first beautiful note of song comes out of his mouth, and the jaws of the judges drop in amazement. What was important was the talent, sweetness, and value of what was on the inside of him, not his outward appearance.

Sometimes we think our efforts aren't worth offering to anyone because we know someone who does it better. If we wait until we have a perfect product to present to the world, or even just to our church family, we'll never do anything in this life. Whether what you do looks "Pinterest perfect" or it's a "Pinterest fail," there is still value in the offering.

Maybe you've said to yourself, "I really love working with little kids, but I know that Sister Sweet and Nice is a great teacher to them, so nobody needs me." Or, "I love people, and I love to study the Word, but I couldn't lead a small group like Brother Been at the Church Forever." Hence, you just sit back and soak in what God is providing for you without stepping out to present your messy gift or your ugly cupcake to the world. I have news for you: Sister and Brother Whoever started out serving while making mistakes, saying the wrong things sometimes, and feeling awkward, but they worked, and they grew, and now you think they've mastered something that you could never even attempt.

You need to start the same way they did. Be available, be open, look for opportunities, and ask your pastor where you can serve. It takes so many hands to do Kingdom work, and many times people are taking on a massive number of roles to make sure that everything is done and done well. We want things to be excellent, but nobody expects perfection. Excellence is giving your best with your whole heart. Everyone loves a gift. Please share yours.

Outside Looking In
(Bella at 2 years)

One morning I took Bella to church with me. The nursery was not yet open when we arrived, so she made the rounds in the church lobby while she explored. Behind a set of French doors there is an area of the children's church where two children were playing with a remote-control toy. One side of the doors was locked in place, while the other side was open to the room where the children were. Bella stood with her face pressed to the glass of the locked side of the doors, watching the kids play. She wandered back and forth in the lobby several times, always returning to that latched door to gaze through the glass and see what they were doing. All the while, just one step to the side would have centered her in the frame of the open door, where she could have just walked on through to have a closer look or a turn to play.

Well, I immediately knew that there was a lesson in that observation for my Sunday blog, but I didn't realize just how timely it was until I heard the sermon for that Sunday morning. Our associate pastor, Scott, was preaching about demonstrating the love of God through serving and how we are to be doers of the Word and not just hearers. He stressed that we need to find our work and our purpose in the Kingdom of God and to get involved in what God is doing instead of just sitting each Sunday morning in a chair, soaking up the music and the sermon, then returning to "life as usual."

Just as Bella only needed to shift her perspective a little to the side to get the full experience of what she was watching, many people need to take one step to move from being an onlooker to a participant. God connects many blessings to our obedience. True love for God demands that we share our gifts and talents with others for their good. There really can be no fulfillment in our lives until we are helping others reach toward what God has for them. If all of us encourage, love, and serve each other, it makes each of us spiritually strong, mature, healthy, and productive.

That step may already be apparent to you. You may know what God is calling you to do, but you've let the enemy tell you that you aren't worthy, that those church people don't want you, that you'd be a hopeless failure at anything you attempt to do for God. It's time to start saying about yourself what God says about you. Read his Word and start declaring to the enemy what is true about who you are.

Maybe you have no clue about where you can begin to serve. You'll need to pray, of course, and start to think about the natural talents and abilities you have and how God could redeem those things for his purposes. Talk to leaders or Christian friends who will encourage you and ask the right questions to help you find that place.

Whether you already know or have no idea, ask about the needs of the church. Start by serving in small things, because there are no small things. What you do may not be seen or recognized, but all the little details that people address in the Kingdom come together to make one harmonious whole that leads people to Jesus—some for the first time, some just going a little deeper—but all of it is necessary. God rewards your faithfulness in doing it.

Quit looking through the glass of a locked door. That lock wasn't meant for you, and it can't keep you out if you just take that one step into your destiny in God.

All of Us

Have you ever visited an Escape Room? There's one in the town where I live, but I have yet to try my hand at this new form of entertainment. However, it's also one of the latest techniques used in education to help students learn how to work in a group while reviewing or learning new academic information. In a technology training last summer, I had the opportunity to participate in an example of this type of lesson.

Last year I tried out a similar activity in one of the classes I co-taught. The students had to work together to solve puzzles, find clues, and decipher codes with no guidance from me. They had to rely on each other, listen to the ideas of their teammates, solve problems as a group, and be willing to try approaches that were different than their own. They had a blast!

After the activity was over, we all talked about how that exercise was like real life. In most businesses and occupations, people rely on the gifts, talents, and knowledge of others to accomplish the objectives of the organization. While the activity and the discussion that followed was good for my elementary students, it brings up an even better reminder to us as members of the body of Christ.

My pastor likes to say that not one of us is as smart as all of us, and not one of us is as strong as all of us together. God did not design us to walk out this Christian life on our own. We need each other, not just to work together to accomplish tasks, but to be there for each other—encouraging, exhorting, teaching, interceding, and serving.

God meant for the spiritual gifts that He gave each of us to be shared. What we lack, someone else can provide to us. What they lack, we can share with them. Every time the voice of the Holy Spirit urges us toward action and we hold back because of fear or self-consciousness, we are robbing our brothers and sisters of a blessing that God desired to give them.

I like the way the Living Bible expresses these verses:

"Instead, we will lovingly follow the truth at all times—speaking truly, dealing truly, living truly—and so become more and more in every way like Christ who is the Head of his body, the Church. Under his direction, the whole body is fitted together perfectly, and each part in its own special way helps the other parts, so that the whole body is healthy and growing and full of love" (Ephesians 4:15-16 TLB).

Are you doing your part? Are you helping in the church where God has placed you? Are you solving problems, searching for knowledge, and contributing your skills? If a third-grader can work in a cooperative group and unlock virtual locks, I'm sure you can be a functioning member of a healthy, growing, loving body of believers, unlocking the promise of God for the corporate body where He has placed you.

Filled to be Emptied
(Bella at 2 years)

Bella spent the night with us and was taking a bath before bedtime. I sat by the tub, and she played in the water. One thing my little one enjoyed doing was pouring water from a container into my cupped hands. She'd pour it out until her cup was empty as the water filled my hands and overflowed back into the tub. When there was no more to pour, she'd take her little hands and push my hands apart so that I'd have to let that last puddle of water in my palms splash out. Then she'd fill her container and continue the game, time after time, until the water got cold and it was time to dry off and get into some clean pajamas.

What a picture of what God wants to do with us! He fills us up to overflowing, and that overflow becomes a blessing to those around us, but when we are inactive, just holding on to the blessing in our hands, he wants us to let it go so He can fill us up again.

It's an old analogy, but I think it bears repeating, that the Dead Sea is "dead" because it is continually being filled but has no outlet streams. Everything that comes into it concentrates there, causing it to be almost ten times saltier than the sea, a condition that means that it cannot support plant or animal life. I've also read that the Dead Sea is receding at an alarming rate. Not only is it devoid of life, but it's also diminishing itself.

I had an opportunity to see "church" demonstrated outside the four walls of a gathering place with a name on the door. A group of Christians met together to minister to a sweet, faith-filled lady and her family as they stood against a diagnosis that may be "fact," but it wasn't God's truth. Those who were in the home were pouring out life to her and each other.

When we don't pour out to others, we become spiritually dead, and we begin to recede, to grow smaller and powerless. Faith, gifts of the spirit, love, compassion—all of these grow by being exercised. Inaction brings stagnation. We were never meant to fill up and then put a lid on what we have received.

"He who believes in Me, as the Scripture has said, out of his heart will flow rivers of living water" (John 7:38). "Flow" means there is movement. We are to do something with what God gives us. We are to be conduits of blessing, love, and grace.

"Heal the sick, cleanse the lepers, raise the dead, cast out demons. Freely you have received, freely give" (Matthew 10:8).

I know that I sometimes tend to get wrapped up in my own little life, and I forget that I have a responsibility to do more than seek God just to meet the needs of my own family. My time on earth should be less about "my life" and more about His kingdom. I'm asking God to show me where and how to flow so that I can freely give as I have received. I know that if I empty myself, He will be faithful to fill me up and give me a new blessing to share once again.

Do They Know?

On the way to church one Sunday, my husband glanced over to his left while he was driving on the interstate and said, "I never knew there was a church over there." My eyes followed his line of sight and saw the building he had noticed for the first time.

His words, "I never knew there was a church..." hung in the air between us for a moment, and we both said, "That'll preach!" I don't know anything about the church family that uses that building. They may be doing dynamic work in our community and seeing salvations regularly. People may be living free and holy lives; the saints may be operating in their spiritual gifts; the leadership may be committed to what Jesus has revealed to them as their mission and vision. Then again, they could be a dried-up, dead, ritualistic bunch of folks who treat the church as a social club. That church on the interstate isn't the point. The point is: I wonder how many people who don't know anything about God are in that state because they never knew there was a church.

In this case it's not a church building I am considering. The church I attend had two church homes before I ever moved to Virginia and has had two more since I became a member. I'm talking about the church as a whole. That's not just my denomination, not my congregation, but the church around the world—the Body of Christ.

How many of us only express our relationship with God within the four walls? Are our churches open to new people? Would a visitor feel welcomed? What about someone who was obviously under the influence or dressed immodestly? Can we reach out in love to them as they are?

We are not just the church corporately; we are the church individually. Are there people in our sphere of influence who don't have a clue what we believe? Are we distinguishable from unbelievers in any way? Are we being the church?

During my teenage years, I had a friend named Melanie, who talked about sharing her faith with others. She would say that she didn't want to enter heaven only to see people turned away at the gates who would look at her and cry, "Why didn't you tell me?"

At the end of the ages, I know there will still be some who have not accepted Christ—those who think that I'm naive or crazy or stupid. I don't care what they think of me, but I don't want to be their excuse for not accepting the truth of God. I don't want them to say that they never knew there was a church. Let's let them know!

Are You Being Used?

I have often heard people talk about God "using them" in ministry. I've heard others say they didn't like the term "being used." Those words usually mean you are generous with your time, talents, or money on behalf of someone who doesn't care about you at all. That person is exploiting you to satisfy their selfish needs and desires. God can indeed make use of us, but His use of our lives is not exploitation but fulfillment.

When a violin is in the hands of an accomplished musician, he uses it for its intended purpose, and the music that results is breathtaking. A paintbrush in the hands of a master painter creates beauty that astounds us. When we place ourselves in the hand of God, He can cause amazing things to happen as we yield our will to Him. The violin and the brush don't work on their own, and neither do we.

"'I am the vine, you are the branches. He who abides in Me, and I in him, bears much fruit; for without Me you can do nothing" (John 15:5).

Abiding—just being continually, persistently, constantly, steadfastly, perpetually—in Him.

A few years ago, my husband and I were house hunting, and we went to view a home that was being shown to us by a gentleman who was handling the sale. We mentioned that we needed a place with a large living area because we hosted a weekly Bible study in our home. We didn't specify our denomination, our doctrine, the topic of our current study—nothing at all. It was just a passing comment. We looked through the home and returned to the living room to find the man weeping. He said, "I can't explain it, but I just suddenly feel convicted for the fact that I've been neglecting the Holy Spirit in my life, and I need to repent for that." We were confused because we hadn't preached, witnessed, or proselytized. We hadn't mentioned the Holy Spirit. All we had done was wander through a house. Of course, we prayed with him and invited him to visit our church, which he did, but the point of this memory is that you don't have to set out to do something for God. He will use you naturally for His purposes when you are just being.

Much of my writing is about my granddaughter, Bella. She is just a normal little girl, growing up in a loving family, who is learning and changing just as she should. She has no idea that God is speaking to me through her in the tiniest little things that she does and says. She makes sure that our family always joins hands and prays before meals, but I doubt that her understanding of Jesus goes much further than that, yet God imparts weighty lessons to me through her almost every week. Bella is not striving to serve. She is just being. In the middle of just being herself, she is being "employed for a purpose," which is another meaning for the word "use."

If you are a member of a church body, you may have a particular formal role in ministry that leads you to expect that God will be using you for specific activities at a church service. Still, you are by no means limited to your title or responsibility. The most significant, meaningful times of ministry that I have experienced were times when I had no plan to "go out to minister." They have been chance encounters when I have been doing very ordinary things. We don't have to work so hard at forcing ourselves to structure ways to reach out. God will set us up for divine appointments and situations that we had no idea were coming.

"...in Him we live and move and have our being..." (Acts 17:28). I realize that's an explanation of spiritual truth. Still, if you picture it in your mind as if Jesus enveloped your physical body, you can see that nobody can encounter you without encountering *Him*.

"He who believes in Me, as the Scripture has said, out of his heart will flow rivers of living water" (John 7:38). It's a flow that comes naturally as an outcome of genuinely believing. We don't have to force the water out, or pump it, or splash it, or carry it; we just need to let it flow.

Catch Fire!

A few weeks ago, my husband and I were driving through a small town in Tennessee when he saw a large tent that had been assembled by the side of the road.

"They havin' a revival?" he asked.

"Nope, just fireworks," I replied, having seen the signs posted along the road.

Then the thought struck me that revival is a lot like fireworks. I don't mean that it should be loud and flashy and short-lived. Far from it! There are some more positive parallels between the two.

Several kinds of materials compose a firework. Gunpowder propels it into the air and causes the explosion. Different types of metals and chemicals such as aluminum, copper, iron, magnesium, and phosphorus create all the sparkle and the color that we see in the night sky. Those things are packed tightly into a cylinder with a fuse. All the potential for the light, the sparkles, the color, and the sound is in that missile. Until someone lights the fuse, there is only silence and darkness.

We're a lot like that. We are packed full of the potential that God has placed within us. We have our gifts and talents. We have dreams of what kind of people we want to be. If we're wise we've packed our lives with Biblical knowledge and training, but unless we apply that spark of the Holy Spirit to our lives, we often stay dormant, complacent, and silent. A firework isn't fulfilling its potential until we light the fuse, and we aren't fulfilling our potential when we get tired, jaded, cynical, or spiritually dry.

We all have seasons of our lives when this can happen. Sometimes it's because of a struggle with circumstances, but other times we can get that way even in the middle of good times in our lives. The important thing is to recognize when it comes and to deal with it. You don't have to attend a revival meeting; you just need to reconnect with the One who revives.

Just like fireworks, each of us has a different expression in the Kingdom when we are living up to our spiritual potential. You might be a sparkler, while your neighbor is a Roman candle, so make sure that you don't expect others' journeys and ministries to be just like yours. Real fireworks have a dazzling array of colors and patterns. We are all uniquely designed for a purpose. Make it your mission to catch fire!

Outgrowing Your Container

God taught me something using a sedum plant—a perennial plant that is easy to grow and hard to kill. I should know, because I usually have a black thumb instead of a green one!

My aunt Glenda gave me this plant at least ten years ago. When she first brought it to me, I planted it in a little white enamel pan. For years I carried that old cookpot with the sedum from house to house as we moved five times during those ten years. I never transplanted it into the ground, because I never knew exactly how long we would stay at each new house. For those ten years, it dutifully turned green in the spring, sent out little flowers in the summer, died back to sticks in the fall and winter, and continued the cycle every year. It didn't grow any bigger, but it stayed healthy and functioned as it should.

When I created a little garden patch around an old tree stump this summer, I finally moved it to a new, larger pot. To my surprise it quickly grew and filled that pot. I had been looking for a tall plant to be the centerpiece of the entire arrangement, and it became apparent that I didn't need to look at the nursery for a focal point for the space. The sedum had grown into that role, and I moved it once again. Again, it shot up several inches and is perfect for the center of this little vignette.

This plant always had the potential to grow and flourish, but I'd kept it almost root-bound in its original container. Once an opportunity for expansion and growth came, it exceeded all my expectations, not once, but twice.

I think some Christians get root-bound. People come to know Christ, and for a while they learn and grow and mature. They find a role in service within the church where God has placed them. However, as the years go by, stagnation happens. They are still productive but have limited themselves to one role—one container—when there are so many more unexplored possibilities for their lives. After stepping into a more significant role, they find that their growth accelerates, and they discover themselves doing things they never imagined. Being transplanted may sometimes even mean a move to a new church home, but at the least it means an act of faith as they expand their sphere of influence.

You can be useful and valuable in your current area of service, but when you are faithful in the things God entrusts to you, there is always an opportunity for promotion and change as He gives you more responsibility and the possibility of unimaginable things in your future. Are you root-bound? As my pastor asked our church family this morning to go after God with a desperate desire, I urge you to seek God for where He is leading you. It's time to grow!

"The righteous shall flourish like a palm tree, He shall grow like a cedar in Lebanon. Those who are planted in the house of the Lord Shall flourish in the courts of our God. They shall still bear fruit in old age; They shall be fresh and flourishing" (Psalms 92:12-14).

When Does Church Start?

At the church where I am a member, we use screens to display announcements and song lyrics, and just before the beginning of the service, there is a countdown clock to let people know when the service will begin. Last week I was thinking about that countdown in terms of the question, "When does church start?"

Church doesn't start when the praise and worship leader plays the opening notes of the first song. It's not the pastor's entrance or the closing of the sanctuary doors. Church starts in each one of us from the day we are born again, because we are the church—people are the church. The building is only a place where we gather. The service is only the appointed time we meet.

So when does church start? It starts at home, when you open your eyes each day and walk out into a world that needs to see Jesus in you. It begins when you are in prayer for your pastor during the week, so he might have a timely word for you and your brothers and sisters when the church next gathers. It begins when those who serve on a Sunday morning are preparing for the needs of the people. It starts in thousands of ways through millions of believers all over the world.

So, if you gather with other believers on Sunday, make sure you are being the church, not just attending a meeting. The Christian life is so much more than putting in a weekly appearance in a building with a church name on the door.

Theme 9:

Relationships with Others

**Practice What You Preach
(Bella at 2 years)**

One summer our family rented a house on the Chesapeake Bay for our vacation. On the street leading to the house was a set of speed bumps. Our granddaughter loved going over them and started raising her hands every time we approached one. Before long everyone in the car was raising their hands, and it created a tradition. It wasn't long before she had us raising our hands as we crossed railroad tracks, went through tunnels, or even turned onto our street, where there is a rough section of pavement. It's become such a family ritual that my husband and I do it when she's not even in the van. (I know, we're weird...)

If we ever forget to do it, Bella reminds all of us as we approach the landmark. "Put your hands up, Mommy. Put your hands up, Daddy. Mamaw, Papaw, put your hands up!"

One day months later, we were riding in the van, and we went through an area behind a store where there were several speed bumps, and later in the trip, we went over three railroad tracks and then went on the street to our house. Bella was so busy telling all of us to put our hands up that most of the time she forgot to raise her own.

I think we can be like that sometimes in our spiritual lives. We give advice or encouragement to others, but sometimes we don't do the very thing we've just told them to do. It's easy just to say what we think is the right thing based on our own experience or Biblical knowledge. We can reduce navigating our journey to a formula of a verse or two of Scripture and a pre-packaged prayer, when what needs to happen is that we follow the leading of the Holy Spirit both in our own lives and as we minister to others.

Even in the life of a Spirit-filled believer, ritual and tradition can overtake the fresh, living direction of the Spirit of God if we are not careful to maintain that connection.

I'm glad Bella finds such joy in childish things, but I hope that she'll remember to focus on her behavior and not on that of others as she grows and matures. The adage "practice what you preach" is still good advice. Examine yourself with me and make sure that's what you are doing.

No More Selfies

Don't be misled by this title. I don't have a problem with people taking selfies, though some people seem to have a real obsession with this that probably isn't healthy. I am the world's worse selfie taker. I never know where to look. I can't get the angle right at all, and I'm not very photogenic in the first place.

One day at work, I left my classroom after lunch to pick up some students and realized that I hadn't refreshed my lipstick after eating, so I pulled the tube from the little pouch I carried with me at school and reapplied it as I walked. Then I used the camera on my phone as a mirror by reversing the view to selfie mode so I could make sure I hadn't overdone the lipstick.

The next day my granddaughter was visiting and was doing something cute (as usual). I grabbed my phone to get a shot of her, but the sight of my own face rudely greeted me. I missed the moment I wanted to capture because the camera's focus was on me.

Then I saw the parallel. When our attention is on our own dreams, plans, problems, and agendas, we miss the needs of those around us.

"Let no one seek his own, but each one the other's well-being" (1 Corinthians 10:24).

"Let each of you look out not only for his own interests, but also for the interests of others" (Philippians 2:4).

"We then who are strong ought to bear with the scruples of the weak, and not to please ourselves" (Romans 15:1).

It sounds to me like God isn't much into selfies, either. I have difficulty keeping my focus away from myself. It's not that I mean to be self-absorbed. It's just that my life is so immediate—so "there"—that I have trouble "seeing around it." I forget to look at how I can be used by God to ease the problems of my natural family and my church family, along with others whom He might bring across my path. God only shows me the shortcomings in my life to help me change them, not to condemn me, so I'll trust that He'll begin to lead me to be more sensitive to those needs in the lives of others and to give me wisdom and insight on how to be a blessing in those situations. Do you need to check your focus, too?

See Them the Way God Sees Them

A few months ago, I walked into the sanctuary of my church and was pleasantly surprised to see someone I had not seen for quite some time. There had been a moral failure in this individual's life, and the details were common knowledge. I was happy to see he was back in church, because I knew that, failure or not, he would be loved and encouraged into a right relationship with God.

I went to tell my husband about seeing this person. My husband is not always great at remembering the names of people. I often need to describe someone's appearance, tell him where the person sits in the congregation, or remind him of an event or a conversation with the person so he can put a face to the description. On this occasion I found myself describing the person by what he had done wrong. Almost immediately, the Holy Spirit reminded me that God sees this person through the blood of Jesus—spotless and acceptable to Him. God sees the potential in his life, the purpose and plan He has for him.

I know that repentance is necessary for forgiveness, and I'm hoping that has already taken place. Still, we as Christians also need to look at those who have fallen with those same eyes of compassion. We need to remember the times that we also have failed. If you described me by my failures and sins, you'd be missing the big picture. You'd be seeing something that is past, something God chooses not to remember anymore. You'd miss the fulfilling vision that He sees for my future.

"For *the Lord does* not *see* as man sees; for man looks at the outward appearance, but the Lord looks at the heart" (1 Samuel 16:7).

I don't know what is going on in the life of this person, but God does, and though the failure may end up being part of a glorious testimony, I resolve that I will not look upon him as the person who sinned but as the prodigal who returned to the Father.

Give 'Em a High Five!
(Bella at 2 years)

I accompanied my son's family to a small local park that featured just two pieces of playground equipment. A young woman was there with her three-year-old daughter and infant son, who was quite content with swaying back and forth in the infant swing, watching his sister play. My granddaughter, Bella, joined the older girl, whom she had never met before, and immediately called her "my friend."

The girls played happily together, climbing up the steps to the slide and going down repeatedly. On one such descent, Bella was at the bottom of the slide while her friend slid down. As the girl reached the bottom, Bella exclaimed, "Good job! High five!" All the adults immediately cracked up laughing because it was so adorable, but it also really touched my heart because my little one seems to be a natural encourager.

We all enjoy the appreciation of others. Hearing someone compliment something we have created, or having someone celebrate something we have accomplished, is a lovely feeling. Last week I received a comment about a post on my blog that not only warmed my heart but also gave me more motivation to continue just doing what I do with my writing. I know my audience is small, and I'm not reaching thousands with my words, but I have heard many pastors say they would preach the same to a congregation of one as they would to an auditorium full of people. The expression of the gift and the obedience in its use are what is essential. I realized through that comment that God is responsible for the expansion of the message, not us.

"Therefore comfort each other and edify one another, just as you also are doing" (1 Thessalonians 5:11).

When you offer sincere words to someone who has blessed you with his gifts and talents, you play a part in the continued flow of what he produces in his life, but don't stop with just the highly visible people. Thank the person who made the coffee, or set the table, or picked up the trash, or any of the hundreds of things people do to make the lives of others better. Talk to the teenagers who are stepping out to attempt something new and give them words that will boost their confidence. Give the senior person some verbal applause for a life skill he has shared with you.

The words you speak may seem insignificant to you, but they could be a turning point in the life of another person. I urge you to look for opportunities to give that gift of encouragement to someone in your life. Make this a priority in your relationships and be a part of letting those gifts flow to others.

"And let us consider one another in order to stir up love and good works, not forsaking the assembling of ourselves together, as *is* the manner of some, but exhorting *one another*, and so much the more as you see the Day approaching" (Hebrews 10:24–25).

Represent!

On one of my school breaks, my husband and I took a four-and-a-half-hour scenic train ride through the Smoky Mountains of Tennessee. We began with a nice lunch in the dining car and then moved to our assigned train car: the cheap seats. The seats were comfortable, but we had opted for the least expensive car, which just had ceiling fans and windows that could open to keep us cool.

We hadn't been seated in the car long when a woman came along with her two friends to sit across the aisle from us, escorted by a coach attendant who asked if this spot was suitable for them. The lady very snidely said, "I guess you weren't listening when I told you I needed air conditioning." The worker explained to the lady that the tickets she had purchased were not for a car that had air conditioning. She continued to complain, and he finally left and returned with the conductor to talk to her about her complaints. I guess they finally got through to her that this is where she would be spending the entirety of the trip, because there was no more interaction between her and the train staff. Her complaints didn't cease. She criticized the staff, the seat, and the scenery. Her grievances consumed the beautiful day.

Why am I telling you this rather uncomfortable little story? It's because the whole time this woman was airing all this unpleasantness, she was wearing a massive cross necklace. My human nature wanted me to go over and ask her to please drop the pendant down the front of her shirt so nobody could see it. I certainly didn't want people to associate Christians with being rude, entitled troublemakers.

Cross necklace or not, if you are known by others to be a Christian, they are watching to see how you treat others, how you react under stress, how you serve your employer, and how you prioritize God in your life. If you are as negative as the world, what is there in your life that would draw someone to Jesus? Are you attracting people to the Kingdom or repelling people *from* the Kingdom?

Her attitude made me check mine. We are walking testaments to the possibilities of how God can transform a life. Let's represent Jesus in such a way that folks can see **"Christ in you, the hope of glory" (Colossians 1:27).**

And God Loves Loopy
(Bella at almost 3 years)

Bella is what most people would call a "character." She talks a blue streak, as they say, and teaches me things every time I see her. Sometimes the lessons are sobering, but this one was a real laugh—at least for a while.

She was spending time in the master bedroom with her Papaw. She knows that if she goes there, he will play one of the shows she likes on his television, even if her daddy is monopolizing the one in the living room.

We can tolerate most of the programs she likes, but there are a few that are so silly or repetitive or boring that we groan as soon as she asks for them. She used to call one of the shows "Loopy" because she got confused about the character's real name. I'll leave it at that so I don't publicly criticize the show. I'm sure he's a perfectly lovely person, but the goofiness of the show grates on the nerves of all the adults in the house.

Anyway, yesterday she was sitting on the floor, watching one of her shows, when she suddenly said to her Papaw, "I like God. God loves me. God loves Loopy." How can you argue with that logic? So, with a groan, he turned to that crazy show, and she got to watch.

She repeated those kinds of thoughts many times that weekend. In fact, on the way to church that Sunday morning, she asked if our pastor, Michael, would be at church. I told her he would, and she said, "I like Michael. Michael loves me." I think she is beginning to connect that love goes both ways and that God's love encompasses all of us.

I laughed over the "God loves Loopy" comment until it hit me that I sometimes forget just how much God loves all of us and how God commands us to love one another. I was venting on the telephone to an old friend of mine about a situation in my extended family. A particular person has caused a great deal of resentment and alienation. I realized that I'd spent more time talking about the pain she has caused than I have spent in praying for her and asking God to intervene in the situation. After all, if God loves Loopy, He must love her, too. Who am I to vent instead of praying? Yes, she is in the wrong. Yes, there has been sin, broken relationships, and lies, but God loved me when I had the same list of strikes on my record.

I'm teaching this little girl many things as she grows, but I thank God that He is using her to teach me, too.

Un-reality Television

On an extended break from school, I'd been watching more television than usual, and I saw many previews for the various "reality shows." I know this is not a new genre in television, but the longer these types of shows continue to be popular, the less I understand why. There is no such thing as "reality" in a reality show. The minute you turn on a camera around a group of people, they cease to be themselves. If you don't believe that, think about the childhood home movies where you and your siblings were showing off, competing for air-time.

The theme of most of these so-called reality shows is how beastly people can be to each other. The fighting, backstabbing, scheming, hissy fits, name-calling, hysterics, and high drama is so over the top that I refuse to believe that this is the reality in which most people exist.

I've lived in several cities in West Virginia and Virginia, I lived in Florida for a while, and I've traveled all over the United States and made two trips to Europe. In all my life, I can count on one hand the number of times I've seen real-life scenes of conflict like that. I hope that the average person in this world wants to live peacefully with others. I guess the evening news, with scenes of war and conflict, could prove me wrong when it comes to the larger political and social issues, but in our personal lives, surely we are not so horrible to those around us.

Have we fallen so far that we think that people can find a mate through a game show competition? Is it now acceptable to be famous just by becoming a single teenage mother? Do we have the mindset that we should win at any price? Is clawing and scratching our way to the top an accurate picture of success? I guess it's a bit like stopping to look at a car wreck. It's horrible, but we are fascinated by the spectacle.

I'm not sure what attracts the American public to this type of programming, but I'd prefer to concentrate on the good in people, not the ugly side of human nature. I think I'll take my cue from this Scripture:

"Finally, brethren, whatever things *are* true, whatever things *are* noble, whatever things *are* just, whatever things *are* pure, whatever things *are* lovely, whatever things *are* of good report, if *there* is any virtue and if there is anything praiseworthy—meditate on these things" (Philippians 4:8).

I don't consider myself a "goody-two-shoes," and I'm not isolating myself from all American culture and media, but shows like these don't make me feel better about myself or other people. When we are trying to live our own lives according to the will of God, doesn't it make sense to concentrate on things that lead us to that end and not on negative thoughts? Let's make sure our reality is treating those around us—in our families, our jobs, and our neighborhoods—with love and respect and leaving a positive mark on those around us every day.

Theme 10:
Difficulties and Challenges

Keep Going Through

When you are walking through a forest, there is no sign in the middle to tell you where you are, so you never know if you are walking into the woods or if you are walking out!

If you are walking through a difficult season in your life, it can sometimes be hard to know exactly where you are in the process. You never know if this is the beginning of a situation or if victory is right around the corner.

In either scenario one thing is sure. If you despair of ever coming out of the forest or out of your current circumstances and you stop, you won't ever come to that clearing you are longing to find.

"My brethren, count it all joy when you fall into various trials, knowing that the testing of your faith produces patience. But let patience have *its* perfect work, that you may be perfect and complete, lacking nothing" (James 1:2-4).

You can't pass the test if you quit before it's over!

Loving Your Enemies

I don't know why I bother reading the comments that people write on YouTube. Almost every time a Christian music video is featured, there are "haters" writing comments about how they view Christianity as an elaborate fairy tale and see all those who believe in Jesus as fools. There is all manner of blasphemy written there. The authors aren't content to just be an unbeliever; they feel compelled to attack those who *do* believe.

At one time I was not overly concerned with the attitudes of these people. I knew one day **"...that at the name of Jesus every knee should bow, of those in heaven, and of those on earth, and of those under the earth, and *that* every tongue should confess *that* Jesus Christ is Lord, to the glory of God the Father"** (Philippians 2:10-11).

I saw that these people would one day know the grave error they had made. Then I realized that my attitude was more about *me* than it was about *them*. I recognized that what appealed to me most about that Scripture was that I would be proven right, along with my brothers and sisters in Christ. We all like to be vindicated. But the Holy Spirit showed me that rather than being smug, I should have an attitude of praying fervently for these souls. These people are so full of hate, so deceived, and so far from the truth of the gospel. I should center my thoughts on their salvation, not their destruction.

I am blessed to know Jesus, whom I have not seen in the flesh, and to believe in His power, love, mercy, and grace. No belief in a myth could have changed my life so completely or given me such purpose and significance. My prayer now will be that those who laugh at me will someday be set free to laugh for the joy of knowing Him.

The Timing of God

My son made the following observation on Facebook once.

"You can be the best hunter in the world, but if there are no deer where you are, then it doesn't matter. You can be the best hunter in the world, but if you arrive in the field at the wrong time, then it doesn't matter. You may feel your God-given talents are pointless and wasted. Remember that you may be waiting to be in the right place and season." — Joshua Ellis

When I read this, I thought of Joseph, dreaming of ruling over his brothers, only to find himself in a prison cell in Egypt. All the promises of God seemed to be made null and void. He was not able to even imagine all God still had in store for him. He had to wait for the right season.

I thought of David, anointed to be king over Israel, running for his life as he fled from King Saul. Did he question the truth of Samuel the prophet's words over him as a young boy as he faced all the adversity? In God's timing he took his rightful place.

Some seasons in our lives are incredibly frustrating. Sometimes we wonder where God is in the middle of our troubles. There were about four years in my life when we were under extreme financial stress. We had just moved to Virginia, and my husband was only able to find temporary work. Within a few months, he developed some health issues that kept him from working at all. We were paying a mortgage payment on the house in West Virginia, which we were trying to sell, as well as a rent payment for our new home. There were times when our grocery budget was less than $25 a week. From a spiritual standpoint, we were doing all we knew how to do, but month after month things grew more difficult. During that time my faith in God grew in a way that it never had before. It's easy to trust God when life is going well, but it's a real challenge when circumstances are burdensome. I wouldn't want to go through that series of events ever again in my life, but I wouldn't go back and change a single thing about that time, because God became even sweeter to me in the middle of all of it. I learned to trust, and I watched as He provided for my needs in ways that, even today, I don't fully understand.

I wrote on my church's Facebook page one day in the worst of the financial mess that I was in:

"Last year I learned so much about faith and patience, about waiting on God, and about trusting His timing. There were situations that I wanted Him to handle differently, but now I can see the 'why' of the way things have played out, the other people He wanted to bless in a situation that I thought was mine alone. Everything we need God to do in our lives also touches the lives of others. Only He sees the big picture. Thank God that He IS God."

The seven years of waiting to sell that West Virginia house ended up being a blessing to the family who purchased it while, at the same time, it taught me to wait and trust. A car that we wanted to sell when it became too difficult to maintain two vehicles finally sold to someone in our church who needed it, and it came at just the right time for him...weeks after I thought I needed to sell it. God's timing is perfect, though we may not always agree with how it unfolds. It's not all about us; it's about Him.

"Wait on the Lord; Be of good courage, And He shall strengthen your heart; Wait, I say, on the Lord!" (Psalms 27:14).

You may be waiting for a financial breakthrough, a ministry opportunity, a restored relationship, a healed body, or an outlet for all your gifts and talents to be used or noticed. If you wait on His timing, you will be assured that all is happening His way and for His glory.

In His Time

When my son and his wife were trying to sell their house, they planted a few fruits and vegetables at our place so they wouldn't have to abandon the harvest if their home was purchased before it was time to enjoy all the produce. The watermelon vines took over a section of the backyard. They started as a few small plants nestled up next to the foundation of the house, but their spreading vines ended up trailing far across the lawn.

One summer day one of them looked ready to eat. It was large and had that nice yellow spot on the bottom that is supposed to indicate that it's ripe. When we cut into it, it looked good, and each of our two families had a large chunk to enjoy. A few days later, in anticipation of a picnic lunch we had planned for a day trip, we thought we'd slice up some more to add to the cooler. My son found one that looked just like the other had looked when we'd served it up. However, when I pulled my large knife across the rind of this one and sliced down to the cutting board, all I saw was a disappointing pale pink color down to the rind. That watermelon got tossed into the woods for the wildlife to enjoy.

To our eyes it looked as if the second melon was ready to serve out its purpose. It looked right on the outside, the time it had been growing indicated that it should be ripe, and our experience before had shown that a melon of that size and appearance should be good to eat. So what happened? It just wasn't time.

I attended a women's conference where the speaker said something much the same. She said that sometimes when we are believing in God for breakthroughs and miracles in our lives, we just need to wait for

God's timing. She said that God's delay is not necessarily God's denial and that He might be waiting for the perfect timing to bring the greatest glory to Himself.

I can remember experiences in my own life when, if God had given me what I wanted at the time, it actually would have been damaging to my situation. God knew the big picture, and His timing was perfect. There are situations right now in my life that I think I see clearly. I know what needs to happen, and I can't imagine why or how a delay in getting that answer could be positive or desirable, but I also know that I don't know everything. In God's infinite wisdom, with an eternal view and a Kingdom purpose, there are reasons I could never comprehend. In the gardens of our lives, He is the ultimate and perfect gardener. He knows when we are ready for the things He desires to give us, the ministries in which He wants to use us in, and the lessons He needs to teach us. It's time to trust the Master Gardener.

"He has made everything beautiful in its time. Also He has put eternity in their hearts, except that no one can find out the work that God does from beginning to end" (Ecclesiastes 3:11).

Does Your Heart Have a Boo-Boo?

Our family has been experiencing a time of testing for many months. After many medical tests and consultations with specialists, my sweet daughter-in-law, Brittney, was diagnosed with a heart issue at the age of 30. Other physical conditions complicate her medical situation. She and my son are dealing with crushing medical debt. She is exhausted and in pain. She's bearing it with grace and faith that God has a plan and that her testimony will be for His glory. I'm believing in her full restoration to health and energy. She needs healing, and our busy little Bella needs her mama.

Brittney had been in the hospital one weekend, and Bella spent a lot of time with me. When we were praying for her mother one night, I asked Bella, "What's wrong with your mommy?" to see what level of understanding she had at this young age. She told me, "Mommy's heart has a boo-boo, and she is at the doctor."

There are a lot of hearts with "boo-boos" in this world. Some are physical heart conditions, but there are many, many more spiritual heart issues than physical. Doctors can treat physical problems. There are medicines, therapies, and surgeries that can improve a person's quality of life and restore health. Still, only the Great Physician, Jesus, can cure a spiritual heart condition.

Just as we seek out medical attention from the doctor who has the right expertise to know what to do in our situation, we must seek the Lord for the healing of our spiritual wounds. If we don't consult the medical experts, our condition may worsen, and it certainly won't improve. In the same way, ignoring God and just expecting our spiritual heartsickness to disappear can cause it to grow worse.

"The Lord *is* near to those who have a broken heart, And saves such as have a contrite spirit" (Psalms 34:18).

In this challenging time for all of us, I'm leaning on God to deal with all the things I am powerless to change. **"Be anxious for nothing, but in everything by prayer and supplication, with thanksgiving, let your requests be known to God; and the peace of God, which surpasses all understanding, will guard your hearts and minds through Christ Jesus" (Philippians 4:6-7).**

Is there a spiritual heart issue that is exhausting you and causing you pain? Have you tried everything else to soothe that discomfort and found that nothing is helping? Consult the right specialist for the job. He created your heart in the first place. He knows what you need, and He has the power to heal every issue in your life.

When It All Goes Wrong

When our son was a little boy, we planned a family trip to Gettysburg, Pennsylvania, to tour the town and battlefields and to witness a Civil War reenactment. Being frugal people (meaning we didn't have enough money for a hotel), we borrowed a tent from a church friend and made the six-hour drive, planning to save money by cooking at the campsite so that food would cost us no more than it would have at home.

Alas, that plan fell apart quickly because the rains came down, day after day, and we could not cook those homemade meals, as it's a terrible idea to use a propane camp stove inside a tent if you want to live to make the trip home. So we did what all good travelers do: We hit the fast-food restaurants! One evening we found ourselves in that traditional Scottish establishment: McDonald's.

One thing that is unique about the Gettysburg area is that, because of the emphasis on history in the town, even the fast-food restaurants are decorated with large paintings by renowned artists that depict battle scenes from the July 1863 conflict there. While waiting for our food, I saw a painting of Pickett's Charge. An ancestor of mine had fought in this battle. I glanced over beside me, and there was a Civil War reenactor in a Union uniform admiring the same picture. We struck up a short conversation, and we found out his name was Mike, and he was from Kenova, West Virginia, not far from where we lived at the time.

Long story short, we exchanged contact information, and when we returned home, he introduced us to the leader of his reenactment group, and we joined the unit shortly after that. Reenacting became a hobby that we pursued as a family for several years. It planted a love of all things historical in our son, which he enjoys to this day. We traveled, learned, made lasting friendships, and contributed to other folks' understanding of Civil War history.

What does all this have to do with anything? Well, my perfect little money-saving plans for feeding our family on a budget were disturbed by the unrelenting rain, but had it not been for the weather, we would not have met Mike, and we may not have experienced this portion of our lives, which we still treasure to this day.

Many times we have our little plans for our lives worked out just so perfectly. We think we are in charge and have it all together, but then circumstances come along that we can't control, and things veer off course. Those interruptions can be just inconvenient or irritating, and sometimes they can even be painful. However, they can lead to something new in our lives that might never have happened had our original plan stayed in place. I think that's what trusting God is all about. We don't always like the path we must walk, but God can bring blessings out of a challenge and make the messes in our lives into messages.

Answers at my Fingertips

One of the things I do as a special education teacher is to read tests aloud to my students so that they can prove their knowledge of a subject without being penalized for their lack of reading ability. One testing season I was reading a math test to a sweet little third-grade girl. Many of my students are allowed other accommodations, such as using a calculator to solve problems. She was one of the students who was permitted to do this.

Throughout the test she was trying her best on each problem. Many only required her to do things like identify the names of various shapes or match vocabulary words to the corresponding pictures. However, others did require actual calculations. She dutifully copied one difficult problem on a dry erase board and began working on it, but she was having trouble solving it. Just a few inches away from her lay the calculator. Due to the rules of the test, I could not remind her it was there. For several minutes she struggled with the calculation, erased, and wrote it again, trying to talk herself through the steps. She even reached over the calculator once to pick up a number line to assist her. Finally, as I held my tongue (and my breath!), she noticed the calculator, looked at me wide-eyed and with a big smile, and picked it up to complete the problem successfully.

Sometimes I am a lot like this third-grader. I take a problem in my life and try to work it out myself. I struggle with the complexities of it, backtrack and try to do it another way, and then I get frustrated. All along, the means to solve my problem is just at my fingertips. Why do we sometimes look at prayer as a last resort instead of the first impulse?

I'm not suggesting prayer always gives us the instant solutions a calculator does, but I do know God's answers to life's problems are always better than ours, even if we don't understand them every time. I'm learning that the first thing I should do is take a situation to Him and then step out in faith of the wisdom He gives me to take actions based on what He has promised. I imagine that when I'm struggling with something on my own, God is patiently waiting for me to remember what is available to me right at that moment and to use the tool of prayer to begin to put things right.

Days of Our Lives

Sometimes the topic of my blog posts comes quite easily. A little event during the week or an overheard phrase becomes an analogy to some spiritual lesson. There are other times that I sit down to write and have no idea what's going to end up online. I must dig a little deeper for inspiration on those evenings, and one such night was a time for digging.

Then I thought about our associate pastor's message from that morning. His title was "These are the Days of our Lives," and no, he wasn't referencing the soap opera. His message was about the different lives we all lead—public, private, and secret—and how we need to let God be the Lord of all those "lives."

My mind took a different direction on that title as I thought about the days of my life. I found an online calculator that told me that, as of that day, I had lived 21,703 days on this earth. Then I thought about how little I remember about each day in my life. Of course, I have vivid memories of my wedding and the births of my children. I remember the day we discovered that our beautiful granddaughter was going to be joining our family. There are scattered mental snapshots of moments on vacation, a few holidays, some painful events, and some profound moments in my relationship with God. For the most part, though, life goes by in lots of ordinary, non-eventful days where I get up, go to work, and come home in a seemingly never-ending cycle. As a teacher I also have a lineup of dull, quiet summer days every year.

I've never been able to keep up the discipline of an everyday diary. However, I do have a little journal, given to me by a good friend, where I have tried to record the significant events in my life. All told, there are less than a hundred days written in that slim volume, but reading over those entries reminds me of some very precious moments and many lessons learned. Because I am learning to hear God in the situations of my life, I can now convey those in writing to share with others. Not all of it is joyful. Some of the events were things that I thought would break me at the time, but running through all of it is the faithfulness of God. He has been in the middle of every circumstance in my life. He used all things "for my good," even when it didn't feel so good at the time.

So much of our lives will be a blur as we move through our daily routines, but every moment is a gift. I encourage you to start a little notebook of your own. Don't put yourself under the bondage of writing something every day, but begin to record the blessings in your life. Write about the funny things your child or grandchild does and says. Record the statement in your pastor's sermon that touched your heart. Pour out your frustrations about a situation, and then write down the outcome that comes after a time of prayer and trusting God. If you aren't much of a writer, at least jot down a word or a phrase, or draw a picture that will remind you of the event. Write the date to help you place that moment in time. Think about how the experiences of the people of the Bible—both tragic and triumphant—serve to teach and inspire us today. Somebody wrote it down.

Ten years of my life are in this little book I've been using, and I've just filled it. When I get discouraged, I sometimes just sit and read about the "roller-coaster" of the last few years and remember what God has done. There's another book in my home office waiting to receive new memories, thoughts, and answered prayers. Let's not let all those "days of our lives" slip through our minds like those "sands through the hourglass." Let's allow the past to give us hope for the future.

Get Rid of the Junk!

If you are a Facebook person, you know how the site will show you posts from previous years on the anniversary of the date that you first posted them. One of mine today was a post from nine years ago that reads like this:

"Packing, sorting, organizing, yard sale planning, weeding out the junk . . . How do people stay organized when they don't move every year, as I have for a while? What will I do when I have to stay in one place for the rest of my life???????"

Ironically, since that move I have moved three more times. Each time there is more accumulated "stuff" that I can easily discard, sell, or give away. If I can live without it and let it leave my life so painlessly, why did I have it in the first place?

I've been thinking about the unnecessary things in my life. I spend some time during each of my breaks from the school calendar going through all my belongings. I let go of the things that I don't need or want. Many of my clothes don't fit anymore. I have books and papers that I'll never reference again. Some kitchen gadgets create more work than they perform. There's no room for all my life's collections of decorative objects and framed pictures. There are a host of other miscellaneous items that just don't have a place in my life anymore. The phrase "less is more" really is true. When I remove the useless, it is much easier to find, use, and enjoy those things that are beautiful and useful in my home.

Just like the physical items in our lives, there are spiritual, mental, and emotional things that we need to release as well. That old resentment against someone in your past? You don't need it. While it is hurting you, they probably haven't even had a thought about you in years. Throw it out. The self-critical attitude you have about yourself? Dump it. God created you to be an amazing piece of work with potential that you cannot begin to comprehend. Fears about the future? Who needs them? God says to "fear not" and to trust your steps to Him. When you discard those old, damaging thoughts and attitudes, it's much easier to find, use, and enjoy those things that are beautiful and useful in your life.

"Therefore we also, since we are surrounded by so great a cloud of witnesses, let us lay aside every weight, and the sin which so easily ensnares *us*, and let us run with endurance the race that is set before us..." (Hebrews 12:1).

An Olympic runner can't race while carrying heavy suitcases, and we can't run our race bogged down by thinking that doesn't align itself with the Word of God. Let's let go of all those "weights" in our lives so we can reach the finish line in our lives in victory.

Because of Who You Are

One of the circumstances that I'm trying to live "over" is my husband's health. He has been having medical issues of several kinds and, a few years ago, was diagnosed with rheumatoid arthritis. Before getting this diagnosis and treatment, it attacked him with a vengeance and moved very quickly. At one point he needed help even getting dressed. He often apologized for being "useless," and he was upset that I needed to help him with so many simple things. I always told him to stop apologizing. I didn't marry him because he was useful. I married him because of the relationship that developed between us. I love him just for being him.

When my children were babies, they were able to do nothing for themselves, yet I loved them fiercely. They were a part of me, and I loved them without them doing the first thing for me.

That train of thought led me to think about my relationship with God. There are circumstances that I've asked God to change that have not changed, yet I still love Him. I love Him not for what He does but for who He is. I love Him because He is the God of the universe, yet He made a way through His Son for me to have a relationship with Him. I love Him because, even though He has not done everything the way that I think He should, He has taken care of me and blessed me in many ways. He is my Father, and I am His child. He loves me when I can do nothing for Him.

In times to come, maybe some of those things that I have longed for will happen. When they do I will be thankful and excited, I am sure, but my joy is a "now" reality, not a "when things are all going my way" dream. However, I'm quite human, and that "joy" is severely challenged sometimes. I've had to fight a mental battle to maintain a right attitude toward God in the middle of all the things I do not understand. Every Sunday, when I join my church family in worship, I'll remember that I am giving God praise just because of who He is while I trust Him with my here and now circumstances.

My joy is not based on my bank account, my health, my job, or even my family situations, but on my relationship with Jesus. I do go through times when discouragement comes, but I am learning to "bring every thought captive to the obedience of Christ" and keep going after Him with everything that is in me (**2 Corinthians 10:5**).

I am believing in a breakthrough in some specific areas of my life, but I don't know exactly when I will see all that come to pass. While I am waiting, I want to publicly say that no matter what is happening in my life, Jesus is everything to me, and He is enough.

When things change, and everything is "going my way" for a season, I don't want anyone to say, "It's easy for her to be happy. She has everything for which she was praying." I had joy before the manifestation of those things. I will have it when I am enjoying my blessings. I will have it when life challenges me again.

Enough is Enough

I am a prolific dreamer. I dream every single night—vividly! One dream centered on a house with a gaping hole in its side. Paul and I stood in front of it, looking at an abandoned, ramshackle house next door. As I scanned the neighborhood, I realized there was no neighborhood. It looked as if there had once been lots, houses, and sidewalks, but they were long gone, leaving just the two homes where I stood. We started to walk across the "lawn," which was a mixture of bare spots and tall clumps of weeds. As I looked down, I saw hundreds of tiny slips of paper scattered all over the yard. I reached down and picked one up, and it said, "Enough is enough!"

As much as I dream, I should be a master dream interpreter, but I've not yet mastered that skill. All I know is that, when I woke up in the morning, the phrase "Enough is enough!" was echoing in my head, and I began to pray. I thanked God for what He was doing in all the difficulties in my life and let the enemy know that everything he had thrown at me in the last several years was not going to accomplish what he intended, so he might as well stop now.

We've had a difficult set of circumstances in our lives for some time now. It's not just one thing; it's a laundry list of issues. In the natural nothing seems to be happening in any of these situations. I've gone through cycles of faith and doubt, hope and discouragement, confidence, and condemnation. That time has also taught me more about God than I had learned in my life before this period. He has matured me in ways that I didn't want to be changed. He has given me valuable encouragement from some beautiful people. Through all these experiences, He has helped me to learn to hear His voice and has taught me little lessons through the most mundane things. Sometimes I've put those thoughts in writing.

I've always known God meant for me to write and had a plan to use my gifts and the insights He gives me. I just had to step out and offer them, but I've balked at committing to writing regularly to a broader audience. I have used every flimsy excuse I could to avoid getting this project off the ground. I have finally run out of ways to avoid being obedient. Even though not a soul may follow my blog or this book, I must write. I guess it's that old "if it only helps one person, it will be worth it" rationale. I know it sounds sappy, but it's true, especially if you are the one person it helps.

When you ask many people how they are doing, they answer, "I'm okay under the circumstances." I've decided that I just refuse to live under them anymore. I'm going to live over my circumstances. I'm going to have joy instead of fear, trust instead of worry, and victory instead of defeat. If you listen to the lessons I've learned on this journey, maybe you'll find something that will help you, too.

Preaching to Myself

One of the things I had the honor of doing at my church at one time was taking notes on my pastor's sermon each Sunday morning and turning them into a study guide for mid-week groups that met to discuss, study, and pray together. As I wrote a summary of what he taught, I wrote questions for discussions that the group leaders could use to get people talking about how the sermon applies to their own lives.

One afternoon, as I finished up the notes, I looked at a discussion question that I had written and realized that I probably wrote it for myself. I wrote this quote:

"Sometimes we think that a life in Christ means that we should be immune from heartache and difficulties. Jesus knew his crucifixion was causing his mother and his disciples pain, but he also knew what the cross was accomplishing and the greater joy that would follow. Can we trust God that a season of difficulty may be in preparation for something greater in our lives?"

After an exciting move to Virginia in 2012, where things worked out beautifully, almost effortlessly, I then had to struggle with problems such as my husband's deteriorating health and some financial challenges. Though I'm an "eternal optimist" and usually make a point of thinking positive, sometimes I felt like God was absent in my situation.

I questioned what I might be doing wrong that might be causing my problems. I prayed and cried and studied and wondered. So, when

I wrote this question, I finally realized that that was one of those situations where God could be working out something amazing for our future through what we were experiencing in the present. If even those closest to Jesus had to experience heartache to have the plan of salvation unfold for us all, how much of the negative in my life may just be a prelude to something extraordinary? If Jesus had spared those people whom He loved from the agony of watching Him die, where would that leave all of us today?

I'm going back to what the Scripture says about praising God in all things. Notice that it doesn't say *for* all things.

"...in everything give thanks; for this is the will of God in Christ Jesus for you" (1 Thessalonians 5:18).

So I thanked God for what was right in my life. I also praised Him for what He was going to do through what was wrong in my life. Don't misunderstand; I continued believing that God would heal my husband and give provisions for my finances, because, through both of those things, we can be more useful and effective in the Kingdom of God. I still claimed and confessed victory. I just quit getting bent out of shape about God's timing.

I asked my friends who interacted with me regularly to remind me of those words from time to time if they saw me developing a bad attitude. We all need someone to remind us of the Word and to encourage us when we have trouble recognizing the working of God in our lives.

I kept this next Scripture taped to my mirror so that I'd be reminded of it every day. It's probably one that you need to remember also. I was excited to see how God would work all things together, and I pray that I will stay true to the calling on my life so that I can accomplish what His purpose is for me.

"And we know that all things work together for good to those who love God, to those who are the called according to *His* purpose" (Romans 8:28).

Theme 11:
Dealing with Being Human

1. Why Do We Rebel?

Human Nature
(Bella at 1 year)

My granddaughter is all of one year old, and she's already teaching me more than I'm imparting to her. Just before her recent birthday party, her mama was planning to make cupcakes. I volunteered to take her to my house for the afternoon because I know just how difficult it is to get anything accomplished with an exploring baby underfoot.

I've done a lot of baby-proofing in my house over the last few months, as she has mastered crawling, but there are still areas that she tries to access that I don't necessarily want her to explore. One of those areas is behind the recliner in the living room, where there is a small trash basket.

So, that afternoon she was happily playing on the floor while I was watching from that very recliner. Eventually, she crawled toward the chair and began to go around the back of it toward a small space between the recliner and the wall, trying to check out that trash basket. To stop that expedition, I put my arm down between her and the basket and firmly said, No!" Immediately, she put her head down toward the floor and began to cry piteously, as if I had just broken her tiny heart.

Bella had a room full of toys chosen just for her. Many other items there were safe for her to explore. Still, she only wanted the one thing that I forbade her to touch. That trash basket held items that were of no worth and some items that could potentially cause her harm, but that was the target she chose.

I began to think about the similarities between her behavior and how we interact with our Father God. He has designed so many things for our good and our pleasure, but in our human sin nature, we reach for the things that have no value and that will hurt us eventually. I'm not just talking about the so-called "big" sins that most Christians avoid; I'm talking about the little things that we put in place of our relationship with God—the useless stuff that keeps us from becoming all that we should. I'm as guilty of this as anyone else I know, so I am not throwing stones.

I have a feeling that I'm going to learn many more lessons through the life of our little one. I hope that you'll remember this little illustration the next time the enemy entices you with something other than God's best for you and that you'll respond to that "check" in your spirit that the Holy Spirit brings when He puts His hand of restraint between you and the things that distract you.

Lock it Yourself
(Bella at almost 2 years)

Since I've had a busy toddler in my life for a while, I've learned there are certain places in my house she wants to explore. I take that back; she wants to explore every space in my house. There aren't enough high shelves in my home to put everything out of her reach, so some cabinets now have plastic locks that keep those curious fingers from digging everything out of that space.

I'm not trying to restrict her curiosity or curtail her freedom. My concern is protecting her from items in my house that could hurt her. She doesn't need to play with glass bowls or small appliances with sharp edges, as intriguing as they might be to her.

During the week, when little Bella is safe at home with her parents, we leave the locks open so that my husband and I don't have to open them each time we need to access the contents of a cabinet. Lately, I've noticed that when Bella comes into our house and heads for the kitchen, the first thing she does is go to those open locks and attempt to lock them herself. She is restricting herself instead of taking the opportunity to get into all that mystery stuff in the kitchen!

God knows that certain things in this world can hurt us. He doesn't use locks to keep us away from those things, though. Instead, His Word tells us to be obedient to Him and shun the evil that would separate us from Him. He gives us free will to choose Him or choose sin.

If we use the wisdom of a toddler when we see situations and temptations the enemy has designed to entrap us, we should engage those locks ourselves through prayer and the Word and, in some cases, by physically walking away from an opportunity to invite sin into our lives. It could be a particular TV network that has programming that you know entices you to watch something that weakens your walk with God. It could be an old friend who invites you to join in the things from which Jesus has already delivered you. It could be any number of open doors where you know what is on the other side.

The Bible tells us, **"No temptation has overtaken you except such as is common to man; but God is faithful, who will not allow you to be tempted beyond what you are able, but with the tempta-**

tion will also make the way of escape, that you may be able to bear it" (1 Corinthians 10:13).

Sometimes that way of escape lies in your own decision making: using wisdom to avoid those triggers that lead you away from God instead of deeper into a relationship with Him. That connection will not only bring joy, power, and strength into your life, but it will also allow you to take those things to those whom God places in your life to influence. Lock those doors!

Rip off the Band-Aid!
(Bella at 2 years)

Have you ever tried to entertain a two-year-old on a three-hour car trip? It's a daunting task. At one point on the trip home one day, Bella turned her attention to a very tiny red mark on her leg, most likely a temporary scar from the last scraped knee incident. She whined that it was hurting and that she needed, as she calls it, a "boo-boo sticker."

My students ask for band-aids all the time, for everything from a hang-nail to a cut so small I can barely see it. Often, they want one just to put over an already well-formed scab that's protecting the skin just fine on its own, in my opinion. "But, Mrs. Ellis, it hurts!"

I try to tell these kiddos that the band-aid will not make the pain go away. All a bandage does is protect the skin while our bodies naturally go through a healing process. There is no pain relief in that little sticky strip.

It's not only children who have problems understanding this concept. I know many adults who are using all sorts of things to cover up hurt in their lives. I've done it myself. People use all manner of things, some destructive and sinful, others just futile and pathetic. We use drugs and alcohol, illicit relationships, excessive sleep, frivolous entertainment, and the pursuit of money—name your poison. All these things are a cover-up to keep us from dealing with the root issue and allowing healing to come, and just like the band-aid, there is no real relief from the pain.

We get so attached to our self-medicating that whatever we are using to mask the issue starts to bring us into bondage, and now we not only have the original wound, but we've created a new problem. We've figuratively dug ourselves a deeper hole.

So what do we do with this cycle of hurt and denial? First you must bring it to Jesus. The Great Physician knows how to deliver healing to us. This kind of healing is a process, not an instantaneous action. Our spirits and souls take time to heal, just as our bodies do. It starts with a surrender to Him and continues through all the channels He uses to make us whole and healthy.

It starts with forgiveness, either by repentance for what you have done or by forgiving someone who has wounded you. It continues by finding out what the Word of God says about the way you should live. The words of the Bible are **"...life to those who find them, And health to all their flesh" (Proverbs 4:22).** You stay in health by learning who you are in Christ, how much Jesus loves you, what amazing plans God has for you, where your place is in His body of believers, and where you can learn, grow, and be accountable to others.

Bella's little childhood cuts and scrapes will all soon heal, band-aids or not, but the big issues in our lives will not clear up on their own. If you are holding an issue, plastering over it with whatever you can to avoid it, please rip off that band-aid and let Jesus bring lasting change and freedom to your life.

Shattering a Miracle

I watched a miracle a few years ago. A family who was broken by sin, addiction, betrayal, and hurt was put back together by the mighty hand of God. After once filing for divorce, they began attending and serving in the same church. Joy was evident in their household. I was amazed at how much was able to be overcome when God was the focus of their lives.

Then, suddenly, it all broke apart. He said, she said—and I don't know who did what to whom first, but they forgot about God, the family was fractured again, and now they are apart.

I can't criticize them. I did the same thing at least twice in my life. I abandoned the pursuit of God and let the miracle that God was working in my life drop to the ground lifeless.

When I was a young teenager, I discovered the reality of Christ beyond the little cartoon pictures of Jesus in my Sunday School papers and became an "on-fire" committed believer, eager to walk out God's plan for my life. Within a few short years, though, I was impatient because things weren't working out the way I thought they should, and I began trying to meet my needs on my own, then fell into a decade long pit of sin and degradation. I ran hard and fast from the calling on my life and made a total mess of things. I had destroyed, by my own hand, the miracle of the discovery of Christ in my life.

When I finally returned to a merciful, forgiving God, I found purpose and contentment and began to walk out my destiny again, thankful for a second chance. But after a few years, I became consumed by my own needs and disappointments again and focused on solving my problems by myself instead of trusting God for His provision. I became a discouraged, defeated, apathetic, nominal Christian who just figured that this "Christian thing" wasn't working for me. I didn't plunge into any gross sin; I just stopped caring. Maybe this way of being away from God is even more dangerous because you tell yourself the lie that you're okay because your morals are still good. Again, I nullified the miracle of the second chance because of my choices.

The fact that I'm writing this now should tell you that I'm back, once again in the center of God's will for me. I've learned that when you begin looking away from God to have your needs met, two things happen. The first is that your needs still aren't met, because all the things you do to fill that void are inferior substitutes that will never satisfy you. The other is that whatever gains you have made cannot be maintained because you have cut yourself off from the source of your life.

Jesus told us to abide in Him. If you abide, you continue in Him; you don't just visit Him from time to time. If you abide, you pursue Him with all your heart; you don't just give him a passing glance. If you abide, you remain grafted into Him as one; you don't live a separate life. **"I am the vine, you *are* the branches. He who abides in Me, and I in him, bears much fruit; for without Me you can do nothing" (John 15:5).**

When you step away from the pursuit of God, you lose the supporting hand that gave you your miracles in the first place. Without that support they fall to the ground and shatter. I am thankful that God is a God of restoration and that He can pick up those broken pieces and put them together once again. This time I have purposed in my heart that, though I will make mistakes, I will never again step away and allow the miracle of my life to come to destruction. I choose to pursue God at all costs, knowing that no cost to me would be greater than the reward of truly knowing Him.

Mind Your Roots!

One evening my husband and I were watching television in our bedroom when we heard an odd sound. I thought someone was dragging something through the gravel in the driveway, but my daughter-in-law yelled to us that a tree had come down in the yard.

The tree that had fallen is not actually within our property boundaries, but it fell into an area adjacent to our lot that we keep mowed and treat as part of our yard. When we went to examine it, we found that this tree had no root system at all. Trapped under the huge trunk were the branches and leaves of a few younger trees that it took down with it on its destructive path toward the ground.

There wasn't a cloud in the sky that evening. The wind wasn't blowing. All was calm and peaceful, but still, with no provocation, that tree fell. It reminded me of all the times that we hear about people who have a massive moral failure revealed or people who do horrific criminal acts. Many times everyone around them is shocked because they considered them to be decent people, friendly neighbors, and even people of faith. Yet suddenly, they fall and fall mightily. Could it be that they had no roots? Were they disconnected even though they gave the appearance of being planted solidly in the community or church?

The tragedy of the fall of people who were once respected and admired is that they don't fall alone. Just like this old, dead tree took down at least two young saplings, so there is collateral damage when a person's sin comes to light. It brings pain to people close to the situation. Those who admired this saint of God are disillusioned. People who are looking for a reason to discredit Christianity respond with cynicism. Someone innocent in the entire situation can sometimes be affected in a way that crushes their faith and moves them from a place of growth to a path of destruction.

Once, this tree was a tall, flourishing part of the woods around it. I don't know what happened to cause the roots to die and leave it without an anchor in the soil around it. What I do know is that, spiritually, that can happen to any of us. If we are not diligent in keeping ourselves in prayer and the Word, we can begin crumbling from the roots even though everyone around us may see us as a "pillar of the church." We can look the part, sound the part, and act the part but still be full of absolutely nothing. Then one day, seemingly out of the blue, we can be swayed by a momentary temptation born of our discontent and fall in a very public and hurtful way that causes a wound to the body of Christ, our family, our friends, and our co-workers. None of us are so strong on our own that we can't fall.

"As you therefore have received Christ Jesus the Lord, so walk in Him, rooted and built up in Him and established in the faith, as you have been taught, abounding in it with thanksgiving" (Colossians 2:6–7).

More than ever we need to watch that we are securely rooted, not for our sakes only, but for the precious brothers and sisters around us, who need us to be strong in the Lord. Mind your roots!

2. How Should We Think and Act?

Cleaning House

I finally realized why I hate cleaning my house so much. It's not the actual work involved. It's not even gathering up all the materials I need or moving objects out of the way so I can get to all the surfaces that I need to sweep or mop or dust or scrub. It's the fact that no matter how hard I work to clean each area, I can never get it perfectly spotless.

This major revelation came to me one summer day as I was doing my "you're on summer vacation from school, so you have no excuse" cleaning. I had swept and mopped a floor, and still, I kept finding small blades of grass and bits of dust in corners and next to baseboards and thresholds. No matter how many fancy cleaning tools and products I buy, my house will never, ever be perfectly clean.

Our lives are like houses. We want to "straighten up" our lives so they'll be beautiful and clean. We make promises to ourselves to start doing certain things or stop doing others, but our willpower isn't enough to make all those necessary changes in our lives. The sin that is in our lives is like those pesky blades of grass and dust bunnies. No matter how hard we try, we can't seem to eradicate all of them. The good news is that God knows that we don't have the power to be perfect, and He has made provision to wash our sin away through the blood of Jesus. We all know that our righteousness is "as filthy rags" (**Isaiah 64:6**), and we are thankful for a Savior who gave His all to make us clean.

I'm thankful for that as well, but this "clean house/clean life" analogy got me thinking. Just because I can never clean this house to perfection doesn't mean that I should put down the brooms and mops and dust rags and just declare defeat. Not having the ability to make my home spotless does not give me a license to just let the filth pile up around me. I am responsible for doing what I can, to the best of my ability, to care for this house that God has given me, to make it a clean, attractive, and healthy place for my family to spend time together.

In the same way, we should not just throw up our hands at the state of our lives and say, "I can never be perfect in this life, so I'll just live any way I want, because Jesus is the one who makes my life clean anyway." We are responsible for living lives that are pleasing to

God to the best of our abilities—to make our "houses" places where we show His love and life to others. I know there are two extremes of doctrine in the Christian world. One says, "Anything goes because grace covers sin," and the other says, "One little slip and God will send you straight to hell." I believe it's a balance. We don't have to walk around in constant fear that we are on the edge of slipping up, but we need to go after God in such a way that our moral lives reflect who we are serving. Living lives free of sin is not a matter of picking up tools to clean up after ourselves; it is a natural outgrowth of letting God change us from the inside out.

Room Enough to Receive It

I am a very organized shopper. I get paid every two weeks, and every two weeks I sit down and plan 14 days of menus and make a grocery list. Now that I have discovered online grocery shopping with curbside pickup, I am saving time and avoiding standing in long lines.

One week, when my husband and I pulled into the pickup lot for our grocery haul, I got out and went to the back of the van to make sure there wasn't anything there to interfere with the store worker loading my bags of groceries. Then one of those little "God moments" occurred as I got a quick analogy about having room to receive what I had purchased.

Sometimes the back of my van holds my granddaughter's stroller or some tools that belong to my husband. If I forget that those things are there, I must relocate them so I can fill the van with those things that I need. Some things I can lift by myself, but other things are too heavy for me to carry, and I need the help of my husband—someone who is stronger than I am.

God has purchased everything for us: salvation, healing, deliverance, power, anointing, strength, peace, joy, and wisdom. Shall I go on? In our lives God desires for us to have all those things that He provides, but there are times when we fill our lives with other things that must move aside for us to receive what He is offering. Some of those things we can brush aside with a simple choice, while others require His strength to lift away. There are times when just talking with a brother or sister in Christ helps to lift those things that are in the way and put them in their proper place.

That was my case at the time of this shopping trip. I had allowed some mindsets to interfere with my walk with God. I had listened to some lies of the enemy, which had discouraged me and made me feel inferior, powerless, and useless. In counsel with a couple who loves me, I began to recognize the root of some of these thoughts, and they helped me to move them out of the way in the spirit so that I would have room to receive the thoughts about myself that God wishes me to have.

What is in your spiritual "trunk" today? Are there attitudes there that you need to set aside? Are there things blocking the flow of blessings in your life that you need to share with someone who knows the mind of God? Do you need to ask God to pick up that heavy distraction and move it out of the way so that you will have a spirit that is open and clear and ready to receive from Him?

Is Your Wood Wet?

As Christians we all go through various seasons and stages in our lives. We have times of great testing as well as times of tremendous breakthrough. We have quiet seasons of rest when there is not much drama as well as seasons of upheaval. We are, by turns, confident and insecure, faith-filled and fearful, joyful and sorrowful, fervent and complacent.

I've recently been in a season that I did not understand. All the circumstances in my life were positive. I had no stressful situations that might tempt me to worry. I should have been thankful for the time of rest between battles. I should've been jubilant and excited, ready to "charge hell with a squirt gun," but instead, I just felt disconnected. I remember a Sunday morning when God was moving in the church service, working in the lives of people, and tremendous joy and excitement was all around me. I felt strangely unmoved, even though I ordinarily would have been thrilled at the ministry that was all around me. It was one of those services when someone could have said, "If that don't light your fire, your wood's wet!"

By that definition I guess that was me, a big piece of wet wood. I sought counsel with a couple from my church, who shared some godly wisdom with me about how to cope with the way I was feeling. I put some of their advice to work, but it was just like a big cloak of lethargy had settled over me, and I had a difficult time motivating myself even to take the steps I needed to take.

One day I was just rolling all these thoughts around in my mind, wondering what was wrong with me. I remembered the "your wood's wet" analogy and wallowed around in that mental picture for a little while, and then the Holy Spirit spoke to me and said, "Wet wood isn't a problem for me." Just that quickly, I remembered the story of Elijah and the prophets of Baal.

The people of Israel had sinned against God by worshipping false gods, and Elijah challenged them to make a choice that day to follow the true God—one who would send the fire to burn up the sacrifice offered to Him. (**1 Kings 18** *tells the story*)

Elijah rebuilt the altar of the Lord, which had been torn down, using twelve stones to represent the twelve tribes of Israel. Then he dug a ditch around the altar, put wood on the altar, and lay the pieces of the bull for the sacrifice on the wood. Then he commanded the people to fill four jars with water and pour it on the meat and the wood. He had them repeat the soaking with the water three times. The water was running off the altar and filled the ditch around the altar.

When the time came for the evening sacrifice, Elijah went near the altar and prayed, asking God to prove that he was the God of Israel and that Elijah was his servant. He asked God to show the people that He was indeed God so that their minds would be changed.

Then fire from the Lord came down and burned the sacrifice, the wood, the stones, and the ground around the altar. <u>It also dried up the water in the ditch.</u> When all the people saw this, they fell to the ground, crying, "The Lord is God! The Lord is God!"

When God Himself reminds you of what He can do, it's much easier to let Him motivate you than for you to motivate yourself. I'm on the way back to a richer, fuller relationship with Him, instead of remaining disconnected.

I know that we live by faith, not by feelings, but often our emotions are signals that we need to examine ourselves to make sure that we are in alignment with God. There will be spiritual highs and lows in all of our lives, but I know a God who can light that fire within us when we've grown weary or complacent or sorrowful. No matter how wet your wood is, God is able!

Detox!

Scrolling down my Facebook newsfeed the other day, I saw an article that quite startled me. It described a special steam treatment to cleanse and detoxify your scalp and hair! Do you mean to tell me that I've been walking around all my life with a toxic scalp? Horrors!

That reminded me how much I see on social media about "cleanses." People do master cleanses, juice cleanses, and vegan cleanses, all to rid their bodies of impurities. The world is trying to purify things of the body while the mind and spirit are filthy.

Why are we so concerned about removing all the toxins from our bodies? Where is the concern for blocking all the negative messages we are taking into our mind, soul, and spirit?

My pastor preached once about how we need to watch who we allow to speak into our lives. Some people will give you permission to back off from the things of God, to stop trusting and following Him. They will insist that you don't have to do "all that" to be right with God. Then there are the media messages that tell you that the Bible is outdated, that Christianity is mean-spirited and not inclusive, that a real, approachable God is a myth that weak-minded people rely on to get by in life.

If you allow all those messages to bombard your mind instead of filling it with God's Word, your thinking will be toxic, which is much more dangerous to your heart than the environmental poisons of the world.

Just as you can't avoid all the toxins in the world that are affecting your body, you can't block all the contamination that comes to your ears from the enemy through media, friends, family, and acquaintances. You wouldn't deliberately ingest a poison into your body, and you shouldn't willingly listen to the voices that attempt to halt your journey to what God has promised.

The Bible is full of warnings about listening to fools and encouragements about listening to wise counsel. God knows that what we hear helps form who we are and what we do in Him.

"So then faith comes by hearing, and hearing by the word of God" (Romans 10:17). Let's let that pure voice be the only one that influences us.

Are You Really Listening?
(Bella at 2 years)

After a weekend of taking care of my granddaughter in her parents' absence, I learned why 60+-year-old women do not have babies. I already knew that raising children is a challenge, even for young people, but a weekend of managing a strong-willed two-year-old showed me the wisdom of God's plan in trusting tiny people with younger parents!

Sometimes my son and his wife say of their little one, "She doesn't listen." I decided that weekend that her problem wasn't a listening problem; it was an obeying problem. Of course, just about everything this kid does points me to a more important lesson, and I realized that sometimes my problem is not listening but obeying.

How many things am I neglecting to do when God has already told me in His Word what He expects? How many times have I felt that nudge of the Holy Spirit to say or do something and used some lame excuse to avoid being obedient to that calling?

When Bella doesn't do what we tell her, it is because she wants to continue to do what she wants. Her flesh says that playing with something dangerous is fun. She thinks it's more important to explore the possibilities of what is in that mystery cabinet than it is to truly listen to what I am asking her to do or warning her to avoid. She's human, and she is two. I will love her regardless, but I will expect her to grow in obedience as she gets older.

In the same way, God will also continue to love us, but He expects us to grow in obedience and understanding as we follow Him. That selfish, self-centered spirit that is in all of us must come under His control and guidance as we pursue Him.

Hunger and Empty Calories
(Bella at 2 years)

Is anybody hungry? That's an easily answered question. From our infancy we recognize the need for food. When we are tiny, we cry for it until someone satisfies our craving by bringing us a bottle. As soon as we develop the least little bit of language, we ask for "milk" or "cookie" or whatever we know how to say to get those hunger pangs under control.

The more we mature, the more control we have over what we put in our mouths. Sometimes we make good, healthy choices, and sometimes we consume junk. We wrestle with our weight and vow to control our diet. Food is a constant in all of our lives. We depend on it for nutrition, and we enjoy it for its taste. We plan, we shop, we cook, we share, and we celebrate—all with food.

God gave living beings the sensation of hunger to ensure that we would seek the food that we need so we could survive. I believe He also provides us with a sense of spiritual hunger to draw us to Himself.

Sometimes, when our family is out in our van, my two-year-old granddaughter passes the time by pretending different things. One of her games of imagination involves giving everyone in the vehicle virtual gummy bears. They are always pink. She gives me some and then tosses them over her head to her papaw and her daddy in the front seat, who pretend to catch them. It's a delightful little game, and we all play along, thanking her for her gift, but her gummies have no taste, no calories, and no nutrition. We don't get any enjoyment or any energy from what she provides to us. Imaginary food profits nothing, even if it's fun.

In our lives as Christians, we sometimes settle for fun things that profit nothing instead of pursuing things that are spiritually nutritious, that provide energy for our lives and, yes, that we can enjoy.

The Bible tells us to "taste and see that the Lord is good." However, we settle for the food of the world that is, at best, bland, and, at worst, poison.

Are you feeding your hunger with empty calories? How is that working out for you? It's not working out too well for me, and I'm asking God to direct my choices so that I am taking in that which He knows will strengthen me and help me grow.

Irrelevant Messages

One night I was searching through my text messages for some information. In the process I discovered many old texts that I no longer needed. Someone had sent a question which I'd answered. A website sent me a password reminder link. A local restaurant offered me a free dessert with my dinner, but that offer had expired. You know, the kinds of things that clutter up your phone.

As I began deleting all the unneeded information, it made me think of other messages in my past. These weren't text messages, or phone messages, or emails, or even written notes or letters. They were the lies of the enemy, which he used to try to circumvent the work of God in my life. Maybe you've heard some of these messages yourself.

"You've messed up too much. You've sinned so deeply that God could never forgive you."

"You'll never amount to much. You don't have anything to offer that church. God can't use you."

"Your mama was that way, and your daddy was that way, and you can't change it. It's just how it is with your family."

"You're not important. Nobody cares about what you think."

"You can never be like that other person from church. You'll never have a relationship with God like they have. God only picks certain people to be like that, and that will never be you."

"God's just waiting for you to mess up so He can cut you off. There's no way you can live right all the time, so you might as well quit now."

Here's what Jesus said about Satan, and these words should be our guide when we hear this kind of venom spewed out in an assault on our minds and spirits.

"He was a murderer from the beginning, not holding to the truth, for there is no truth in him. When he lies, he speaks his native language, for he is a liar and the father of lies" (John 8:44 NIV).

Jesus spoke the definitive word on the sayings of the enemy. Don't believe anything he says, because he is a liar. Don't even entertain those messages for a moment. They come from the source of lies, and there is no truth in them.

We know the enemy hates life. He especially detests the lives of those whom he knows are the saved, the called, and the chosen of God. He murders reputations, hopes, callings, dreams, relationships, and ministries—anything birthed of God and His promises in our lives.

So, just like I scrolled through my phone that night, deleting all the irrelevant texts, take authority over those messages that he's been trying to sneak into your mind and heart and begin to attack with the only weapons God gave you: the sword of the Spirit and the Word of God. Blow up his "phone" with these messages:

"God says that He has redeemed me, called me by name, and I am His."
– based on Isaiah 43:1

"God says that if I confess my sins, He'll forgive me and make me clean."
– based on 1 John 1:9

"The Word says that the manifestation of the Spirit is given to each one, so that means me. Those gifts are to profit everyone, so I know God has gifted me to give and serve in His church and His Kingdom" – based on 1 Corinthians 12:7

"God doesn't have favorites. His blessings of eternal life, glory, honor, and peace are for everyone who works with what is good." – based on Romans 2:7–11

"God says I am a new creature. My old life is gone!" – based on 2 Corinthians 5:17

That's just the tip of the proverbial iceberg of the things that a God who cannot lie says about you. Dig into the book and see what messages you should keep close to you forever and never delete.

Perception or Deception

On one of our family vacations, we rented a little house as a base of operations for our beach trip. The home was next to a nature preserve, and the beach was undeveloped—no hotels, no stores, no restaurants. One morning we headed to the beach early because the weatherman was predicting thunderstorms later in the day.

As I approached the water's edge that morning and the first little waves washed over my feet, I jumped back from the initial shock of the cold. At that point, if it had been up to me, I would have retreated to the warm safety of the beach blanket, but a certain little girl wanted to play in the ocean, so I had to keep venturing out.

After a few minutes of wading just ankle-deep, the temperature didn't seem quite so bone-chilling. Little by little I walked farther out into the water, until the water no longer seemed that cold but rather refreshing and pleasant.

I've noticed that in our culture there are things that, at one time, were shocking to hear but are now quite commonplace. The first introductions of those subjects were like a symbolic slap in the face to the mainstream of our culture, but as the media continued bombarding us with the same messages year after year, the average person began to become accustomed to the so-called "new normal," just as I got used to the temperature of the ocean water. In some cases, not only the culture but the church herself also began to retreat from what the Word of God teaches and began to conform to the world.

I fell into this very trap myself in my late teens and early twenties. I remember being in the middle of my sinful lifestyle and being so angry with people who wanted me to act in a more conventionally moral way. I used to consider those people to be closed-minded. Now I know that it's possible to be so open-minded that your brains fall out!

The temperature of the water in the ocean that morning didn't change one degree in the short time I was wading. Only my perception of the cold changed. God's Word does not change. It's up to us to place ourselves in agreement with what He says instead of expecting Him to "get with the times." Make sure the perceptions you have of this world aren't just deceptions of the enemy.

Driving with My Eyes Closed

I don't often take an afternoon nap, because it makes it difficult for me to go to sleep at bedtime, but one day the couch was beckoning, and I took a daytime snooze. Just before I woke up, I had a dream where I found myself suddenly in the driver's seat of a car on a busy highway. I could hear the voice of that annoying GPS lady telling me to move to the left turning lane. The problem was that I could see absolutely nothing. My eyes were closed in the dream, just as they were in real life as I slept. In the dream I knew that I was asleep, and I was desperately trying to wake up and open my eyes so

I could see where I was going, but I was so sleepy that there was no way my eyes would open, despite my panic. I wanted nothing more than for someone else to take control of the car because I had no information to guide me to keep me from causing an accident.

This dream shook me a little. On a natural level, it would be a terrifying experience, but when I thought about the spiritual applications, it was equally as scary. I know there is an area of my life where I have been asleep. I've chosen to hit the figurative snooze button and ignore the information that I need to make a course correction. I've closed my eyes spiritually instead of letting the Holy Spirit take control of the journey, giving me step-by-step directions. The difference is that in the dream, no matter how hard I tried, my eyes would not open. In real life I've chosen to close them.

All blindness is not physical. In the gospels we read about Jesus giving sight to the blind. The Bible also talks about bribes blinding the wise and blind teachers leading others into error. Jesus called the Pharisees blind guides. The epistles speak about minds being blinded. In the book of Revelations, Jesus says to the lukewarm church: **"I know your works, that you are neither cold nor hot. I could wish you were cold or hot. So then, because you are lukewarm, and neither cold nor hot, I will vomit you out of My mouth. Because you say, 'I am rich, have become wealthy, and have need of nothing'—and do not know that you are wretched, miserable, poor, blind, and naked—I counsel you to buy from Me gold refined in the fire, that you may be rich; and white garments, that you may be clothed, that the shame of your nakedness may not be revealed; and anoint your eyes with eye salve, that you may see. As many as I love, I rebuke and chasten. Therefore be zealous and repent. Behold, I stand at the door and knock. If anyone hears My voice and opens the door, I will come in to him and dine with him, and he with Me"** (Revelation 3:15-20).

Jesus wasn't talking to the unsaved in that "knocking at the door" Scripture. Jesus is talking to His church. To us—to you and to me. Now is the time to confront and deal with any area of spiritual blindness in your life. Jesus never healed anyone who didn't desire to be changed. I've heard people say that the Holy Spirit is a gentleman and that He won't force anything in our lives. We must be willing. Today I am willing to open my eyes and quit driving blind. How about you?

I Wish I Was or I Wish I Were?

There are so many customs humans have when they want to wish for something: blowing dandelion fluff, blowing out birthday candles, pulling the turkey wishbone, crossing their fingers, or finding four-leaf clovers. You could probably add something else to this list.

The other day I indulged myself in watching the musical version of *Cinderella*, which was often on television when I was a child. In the story all the girls in the kingdom are hoping to become the chosen bride of the prince, and they are wishing they were older, or younger, or sweeter, or bolder, or any of the other traits they don't have that cause the prince to disqualify them from having their dream fulfilled.

That's been the story of my life for quite some time now. It's not that I want to marry a prince. I married mine over 33 years ago, and I thank God for him. My wishes are of the self-improvement kind. I wish I were a person who kept better track of my checking account or flossed every day or could lose weight AND keep it off. As a Christian I wish I were a person who studied the Word more or prayed more or reached out to people more naturally.

I started thinking about the was vs. were and just could not remember my high school English teachers addressing the rules when it comes to these types of phrases. So, like any modern person, I did an internet search. I found a variety of opinions on which is correct, but one of the most interesting things I found is this: One should say, "I wish I were" when the goal they are hoping for is impossible or highly improbable. An example would be me saying, "I wish I were 21 years old and five feet and eight inches tall." Those of you who know me are aware that I'll never see 21 again, and I have never even glimpsed five feet and one inch. It's just not going to happen.

The phrase "I wish I was" is reserved for those things that are approachable. In my case most of the things I genuinely wish for are possible, but most of them require some action on my part. How do I get to become a person who does all those things? Well, the people who do those things are the people who decide to do them and then follow through. Every day I do the things I have to do, like go to work, but in my free time, I end up doing what I want to do instead of the things I should.

I am one decision away from everything I want to change in my life. I can't do any of it on my own, but with God's help I can be successful. However, God won't force me or do it for me. His Word says that God's divine power has **"...given to us all things that *pertain* to life and godliness..."** (2 Peter 1:3). I don't have to wait for anything to begin making those changes in my life. It's one of those "one foot in front of the other" kinds of beginnings. What do you wish for yourself? Let's take some first steps, and the sooner, the better!

3. What If I've Messed Up?

Never Too Late

"You've ruined your life."

Those are the words of my father, over 40 years ago, when he learned that I was pregnant. I was 19 years old, single, and a college student. I don't blame him for thinking this way. I was the girl "least likely" to get pregnant in her freshman year at college. If people from my high school had predicted my future, they would have said that I would become a minister, not a single mom.

The reasons I found myself in that situation aren't all that important anymore. I took full responsibility for the decisions that brought me to that place, and with the support of a wonderful grandmother, I gave birth to that child and made a life with her. My father died when she was six months old and never got to see what happened next.

Did he think that I'd never finish my education, that no decent man would ever marry me, that I'd never have a career, that my relationship with God was over? I wonder…

In retrospect I think his words were a blessing in disguise. They spurred me to prove him wrong.

By the time my daughter was four years old, I had returned to college and graduated with a degree in education. When she was eight years old, I married my husband, Paul, and he adopted her. Now we have passed our 33rd wedding anniversary, have a wonderful son and daughter-in-law, and have recently welcomed our first grandchild. I've taught for 36 years and have been able to make a good living. My relationship with God is the most rewarding part of my life, and I'm actively involved in my church. My life is full and rich and rewarding, not ruined at all.

I just don't believe in ruined lives. I think there is always a choice to make a change and that the grace of God is available to move that choice into reality. People who have abused drugs and alcohol get clean and sober. I've heard of criminals going straight. Promiscuous people become faithful spouses or celibate singles; gossips become friends who keep confidences; gluttons gain control; abusive people become loving and nurturing. All of this is possible. Even someone whose choices have given them a lifetime prison sentence can choose to live a blessed life within that situation.

"Therefore, if anyone *is* in Christ, *he is* a new creation; old things have passed away; behold, all things have become new" (2 Corinthians 5:17).

That scripture works whether you are just entering the Christian life for the first time or whether you've been there and let your decisions take you in the wrong direction. Grace forgives, covers, and gives you a new beginning, whether you are 19 or 49 or 89. If you know someone who is self-critical and despairing of ever making their life work, please share this story with them. Please tell them that it is never too late.

Altered at the Altar

I have been a special education teacher for over 30 years. I have mastered the art of reading upside down when I am sitting across the table from a student. I have deciphered more convoluted spelling than you have probably ever seen and made sense of the ideas my kiddos were trying to write. I've also edited the work of adult writers and found all the small errors that some people wouldn't even notice. I'm not a perfect writer myself, and I'm sure others could find fault in my writing, but I do think that my spelling and word usage are usually accurate.

Several weeks ago I saw someone's Facebook post talking about the beautiful things that God had done that morning in their church at the "alter." The teacher in me mentally took out my red pen to mark the incorrect usage of the homonym for "altar," but then the Holy Spirit stopped that train of thought in its proverbial tracks. It may have been a technical error, but spiritually, it was very accurate.

In the Old Covenant sacrificial system, an altar was a place where the priests sacrificed animals to cover the sins of men. The animals were a substitute so that people did not have to give up their own lives for the wrong they had done. Rather than getting what they deserved, they offered the blood of the sacrifice.

The New Covenant is built on Jesus being the sacrifice once and for all. The cross becomes our altar—the place where He became the ultimate, perfect sacrifice and took away the sin of the world. We don't get what we deserve, because Jesus took on Himself the penalty of the death we deserved.

When my friend talked about the "alter," it struck me that his word choice was a picture of what should happen at the "altar." In the Old Covenant, in the formality of the sacrificial system, sin was covered, but I'm not sure the ritual ever changed many individual lives. In the New Covenant, God makes it clear that we are new creatures in Christ. When an encounter with God happens at the altar today, our lives can and should change.

"Therefore, if any man *is* in Christ, *he is* a new creation; old things have passed away; behold, all things have become new" (2 Corinthians 5:17)

I know that sometimes I have been guilty of going to the altar to make some whispered promises to God that I have not kept. Real transformation means allowing the Holy Spirit access into the deepest places in our hearts and being obedient as He directs us.
"But be doers of the word, and not hearers only, deceiving yourselves. For if anyone is a hearer of the word and not a doer, he is like a man observing his natural face in a mirror; for he observes himself, goes away, and immediately forgets what kind of man he was" (James 1:22–24).

I remember a special morning when my church had a baptismal service that was more than just a religious ritual. It was a celebration of all the amazing things that God had been doing there. It was a demonstration that the lives of people had been "altered at the altar." I heard stories of bondages broken, marriages and families restored, lives transformed, and purposes discovered. That's what is supposed to happen. I hope it is happening in your life and your church. As it does the church at large can begin to touch the world with the power of God.

The Father of Scammers

Like many folks these days, I seldom answer my phone if the number calling is not in my contacts list. Now telemarketers and scam artists can call from anywhere in the world while displaying a number that looks as if it could be your next-door neighbor's. It's wise just to ignore unrecognized calls and hope that if it truly is a legitimate call, the caller will leave a voicemail message.

The other day I received a call like that. Most of the time, the scammers don't leave a message, but this time I got a notification that I had a voicemail. It went something like this:

"You will be taken under custody by the local cops. There are four serious allegations pressed on your name at this moment. We would request you get back to us so we can discuss this case before taking legal action."

Sounds legitimate and scary, doesn't it? I'm sure that if the local constabulary were on their way to arrest me, they would call to warn me first so I could get out of town before their arrival!

Of course, like any internet savvy person, I typed the words "four serious allegations" into Google and read about the type of scam these people were pulling. Of course, it's an attempt to scare folks into paying money to the scammer to avoid arrest. I also got an email recently that prominently displayed a password I used to use a lot in the subject line. That scammer really had obtained that password from a data breach with my health insurance company and used it to threaten me with exposure, saying that they had control of my computer and had a split-screen video with my face on one side and the porn site I was allegedly viewing on the other. Of course, for a fee they would agree not to send this video to all my email contacts.

Of course, in both cases I knew I was innocent of anything the scammers were trying to pin on me. Other people may have enough guilt in their lives to believe there might be some truth in these threats, and so they pay money to avoid the malicious actions these criminals are using as intimidation.

Satan is like that.

Even as followers of Jesus, we will sometimes fall into sin, make mistakes, lose our tempers, or say something unkind to someone. We are not perfect and will not be this side of heaven. Even a nonbeliever has a conscience, and our consciences will tell us when we've done something that isn't in line with our moral code. If we are walking in a close relationship with the Holy Spirit, He will gently rebuke us for our choices, but it is a loving rebuke meant to bring us into closer fellowship with God and to shape us into the image of Jesus. The Holy Spirit won't bring an accusation with a threat of condemnation, but there will be conviction with a promise of mercy and grace.

The enemy's accusations mean to bring us into a place of shame, a place where we will avoid fellowship with God because we feel unworthy. In ourselves we are unworthy, but Jesus paid the price to bring us into a position of wholeness, cleanness, and right-standing with God. **"If we confess our sins, He is faithful and just to forgive us our sins and to cleanse us from all unrighteousness"** (1 John 1:9).

Many times Satan will bring an accusation against you that isn't even true, but because he is the father of lies, he'll put enough truth with the lie to make you question whether you were wrong in a situation. Ask the Holy Spirit to show you the truth.

Don't let that scam artist deprive you of fellowship with God. Don't let him steal from you all the blessings God has given you. Don't give him permission to speak into your life and rob you of your joy. Don't answer back to him when he delivers a false accusation. He just isn't worth your time.

A Safe Distance from the Altar

I once went to a revival service in a little country church where my pastor was preaching. The message was powerful, and the time of altar ministry was sweet. As the service ended and people began leaving the sanctuary, my pastor turned and pointed to a lady standing next to me in the aisle. He said to her, "God is after you!" Then he turned and began to talk to someone else. What she said to me after he turned away has made a significant impact on me, so I've written her a letter that I want to share with you.

Dear "Lady from the Revival,"

When my pastor turned to you after the service this evening and said, "God is after you," you said to me, "I'm staying a safe distance from the altar." We chatted as you stood to wait for your sister, and you said you used to serve God, but you weren't living for Him now. I said that I had also done that at one point in my life. Maybe I should have said more, but people were milling around the room, gathering their belongings and their children so they could exit the building. It just didn't seem to be the right time to pursue the subject with you, but what you said has stayed on my mind for all the hours since I heard it.

You see, I may not know what caused you to walk away or what sin you think keeps you from coming back, but I do know what it's like to run from a calling, and I know what it's like to avoid being in a place where you might have to acknowledge your need to turn back to God and His plan for your life. I remember wanting to do things my way and feeling that all those people who were urging me back to God were just being narrow-minded. Later in my life, I remember feeling that I'd messed up too much and degraded myself far beyond God's willingness to restore me, so there was just no use in coming back to Him. There were a lot of wasted years when I could have been making a Kingdom difference, but I was living a frivolous, shallow life.

Then one day I found myself in a church service, much like the one where I met you. I realized I could not make changes in my life without a true transformation—one I was not capable of making on my own. Instead of staying a safe distance from the altar that night, I made my way to the safety of a loving Father, who began to make all things new.

When you said you were staying a safe distance from the altar, you said it the same way a woman on a diet says she's going to avoid going to a candy store or like how a shopaholic who is trying to break a spending habit says she isn't going to the mall. It's not because you don't want what is there; it's because you *do* want what's there, and you know that if you get that close, you won't be able to resist the pull of the presence of God any longer.

It boils down to this: The altar is the only safe place there is in this world. It's not necessarily a physical altar, but it's the altar in our hearts, where we lay down our "stuff" and allow God to do His work in us. What is it that you are holding on to that makes you safer where you are than in His loving arms? What do you think will happen if you return to Him? Are you afraid that you will finally fulfill His purpose for you? Don't you know that until you find that purpose and walk in it, you will never truly be satisfied with anything in this life?

If you walked with Him once, you must have heard this scripture:

"For I am persuaded, that neither death, nor life, nor angels, nor principalities, nor powers, nor things present, nor things to come, Nor height, nor depth, nor any other creature, shall be able to separate us from the love of God, which is in Christ Jesus our Lord" (Romans 8:38–39 KJV).

The only thing separating you from His love right now is your choice to keep Him at arm's length.

Nothing else.

I'm not so arrogant to think that my few simple words here would be persuasive enough to bring you to a place where you would run back to that altar of forgiveness and acceptance, but I will be praying that you do just that. Sharing the gospel can be as simple as telling others the good news of what God has done for us. So, when He lifts you back up after you surrender again to Him, do the same for someone else. Share your story and point them back to safety.

Love,
Jan

Saved for a Purpose

On Bella's second Christmas, just before she turned two, she was in awe of the Christmas tree in my living room. However, it didn't look so lovely the morning before she saw it. We bought this tree a few years ago because it was pre-lit, which sounds great in theory but not so much in practice. After a couple of Christmas seasons, it had begun to look at little worse for the wear.

The trouble with pre-lit trees is that sometimes one or more strands of the lights that are attached will burn out. In this case the top and bottom of the tree were glowing, but the middle section was a black hole. Not only that, but I think this tree was related to the Charlie Brown Christmas tree. There was no mistaking this one for a real tree, because the branches were sparse, and you could see through to the center of the tree, and it in no way resembled an actual tree trunk.

Anyway, as we set the tree up and added a set of lights to the dark center, my husband said that we were getting too old to put up with having things that didn't work, so in his opinion it was time for the tree to be tossed and replaced. A day or so after Christmas, I found an unlit tree that looked very realistic, and it was marked down almost 70%. Some light strings were on sale as well, so out with the old and in with the new!

That brings me to the disposal of the old tree. Rather than taking it to the landfill, I decided to advertise it on some of the Facebook yard sale sites as a freebie. Within minutes I got a text from my friend Scott, who thought he could use it in his business office. Now, I had been very candid in the Facebook ad about all that was wrong with this tree, so I asked him, "Do you want it even with its imperfections?" Almost as soon as I sent the text, I thought the same thought that he texted back to me: "Sounds like a good sermon or your next blog topic."

I guess he was right, because here it is. Aren't you thankful that in your life God is more like Scott than like me? (At least as it pertains to our attitude about this tree anyway.) The world rejects us when we are not performing the way it thinks we should. The enemy is always whispering in our ear to convince us that we aren't worthy of anything. He magnifies every flaw, picks at every failure. But just like Scott was willing to take the tree and let it continue to serve a purpose, Jesus accepts us with all our imperfections and makes something beautiful out of our lives, if we will allow Him to.

This tree will adorn Scott's office next year. He may take the time to add some additional greenery to fill it out a little. Lights will sparkle in the dark spaces. Fancy ornaments may decorate the branches. He'll make something lovely out of something that I rejected. He kept it from being discarded, but he kept it for a purpose. Jesus didn't just claim you to keep you out of the landfill of hell; He also claimed you to put you to use here—in His business office called planet Earth. Make it your priority to function as He has designed you and to discover what purpose He has for you.

"Brethren, I do not count myself to have apprehended; but one thing I do, forgetting those things which are behind and reaching forward to those things which are ahead, I press toward the goal for the prize of the upward call of God in Christ Jesus" (Philippians 3:13-14).

It's All Past

I once saw a Facebook post quoting some song lyrics that pertained to being redeemed and not being who we used to be. As I thought about that, I realized that most of the time, when we think about someone's redemption, we think about a person's past in terms of who he was before he met Jesus, but really, our past is any moment before the one we are in right now.

I don't know about you, but I am far from perfect, and I make mistakes every day. There are areas of my life where I disappoint myself. I have goals and expectations for myself that I have not yet reached. Yet, in other ways I have come so far from the person I used to be that I barely recognize the woman in the mirror sometimes.

Many times people say that "Jesus died for our sins—past, present, and future." Many people take that truth as a license to sin. We should be motivated to live a holy life in gratitude for all that God has done to have a relationship with us. Your past isn't just the time before you prayed a prayer of salvation. It's also every moment before this one. Every moment is part of your past that Jesus died to redeem.

"Dear friends, you always followed my instruction when I was with you. And now that I am away, it is even more important. Work hard to show the results of your salvation, obeying God with deep reverence and fear" (Philippians 2:12 NLT). In those times when we do fail, we have this promise: "If we confess our sins, He is faithful and just to forgive us our sins and to cleanse us from all unrighteousness" (1 John 1:9).

Here's what I know. I celebrated my 61st birthday this year. That's a lot of past. There's a big chunk of time when I was rebelling against God and running as far and as fast as I could from the calling that I knew was on my life. There are stories of that time that I could tell you that would "curl your hair," but all of that is past. There are countless other stories of little things that most people wouldn't even consider to be wrong that I know are failures for me, and still, God has forgiven those things and put them in my past, even those that may have happened just today.

The only direction we can ever walk is into our future. I am so thankful that God holds past, present, and future in His hands, and He has plans for me that I cannot even imagine and grace for me as I grow into those plans and purposes. I can walk redeemed every day if I continue to pursue God through all the circumstances of my life.

Renovating Your Soul

When we moved into our new house, the bedroom I chose for my office had previously been a haven for a teenage boy. The walls were a battleship gray color and needed a fresh coat of paint. I promised myself I would update the color in the spring.

My husband and I finally took on the project of sprucing up that office, and I remembered why I hate painting.

First there is all the prep work—gathering the supplies, moving the furniture, taping off door and window trim, filling nail holes with spackle, and on and on...

Then you begin cutting in around the doors and windows with the brush, and at first it looks terrible! Even though the new color is fresh and light, it doesn't always cover well on that first coat, and you're sure you'll need to paint multiple coats. The old color looks ugly and dull, and you simultaneously wonder why you didn't cover it sooner and why you ever even started this project in the first place.

Next there is the task of rolling paint onto the walls, followed by wiping up all the little drips that you manage to leave on the hardwood floor. Finally, when you think it's as good as it's going to get, you must peel off all the painter's tape, wash the brushes, and put up all the supplies. Overall, the whole job is a giant pain in the neck.

You can finally walk away from the mess and take a break because you know there is nothing more boring than watching paint dry. After a while you get enough energy to return to the room to put things back in order, and something extraordinary has happened. The room has an entirely different personality, and the color choice has changed the atmosphere of the space.

If I haven't lost you in the tedious details so far, I'll explain why I wrote them. The Holy Spirit has a way of using these mundane events in my life to talk to me. As I started this hated project that morning, He began to draw some parallels for me.

When we give our lives to Jesus, He begins to change us. He takes that ugly, dull soul and begins to change it into something beautiful. We are partners in that metamorphosis as we yield to Him and start our job of following where He leads. The Holy Spirit was showing me that the transformation process is a lot like painting a room. When you first begin, you can see yourself for who you are. You see your sin and your inadequacies. You magnify your human faults in your own eyes. That little bit of beauty that He paints on your soul at first shows you just how unattractive your inner man was by contrast.

During our years on earth, after we are born again, we are in a constant process of sanctification—being set apart and dedicated to God above all else. The process can be messy and tedious. It's not all glory and shouting. There are spiritual "nail holes" in our lives that we need to fill with spiritual "spackle" in the form of the Word of God. There are times when it isn't easy to continue to follow, and sometimes you wonder why you ever started down this path in the first place. If you continue, though, you'll eventually begin to see the transformation that He has been doing come into clearer focus. Though none of us will ever see the whole picture completed in this life, we can see where He is headed with our lives if we get close to His heart and begin to see the "room" of our soul through His eyes.

"Therefore if anyone is in Christ, he is a new creation. The old has passed away; behold, the new has come" (2 Corinthians 5:17 ESV).

Final Thoughts

The 20th House

When my husband and I had been married for 29 years, we had lived in 20 different houses. I read somewhere that the average American moves 11 times in his lifetime, so we are well above average. I guess everyone needs to excel in something!

Those 20 houses represent life in three states, jobs in five school districts, involvement in four churches, and relationships with friends, co-workers, and church family too numerous to count. I have learned many lessons through all those houses. The circumstances surrounding how we came to live in each one tell a variety of tales.

I even dream about houses! I don't mean that I sit around and daydream about designing my next house, but I literally have recurring dreams about houses, each dream unique and vivid. I believe God speaks to us in dreams, so I've thought and prayed about those night visions to look for what He might be trying to say to me through such a powerful symbol in my life, given my vagabond history.

I don't presume to teach on the dream symbolism or literary symbolism of the image of a house, but many dream interpreters believe that often a house is a symbol for one's own life. If so I have lots of dreams to wade through to find the applications of these to my life.

As I sit in this 20th house, I know I'm probably not finished with moving. I also know that my spiritual house will still be changing and that there are many possibilities in my life that I can explore, and I believe that the things I am learning are not unique to me.

"For we know that if our earthly house, this *tent*, is destroyed, we have a building from God, a house not made with hands, eternal in the heavens" (2 Corinthians 5:1).

We are all a house made by God, and if we allow Him, the Holy Spirit inhabits our house. I hope as you shared my life through this book, you discovered some things He has destined for your life to be until you move into that building from God, a house not made with hands, eternal in the heavens. That's the last move we'll ever make!

The 21st House

Yes, we moved into the 20th house, but we didn't stop there. In October of 2016, we moved to House #21. Yes, we've packed up everything and done this thing all over again.

I have learned not to proclaim that any move is the last move, but I'm hoping that's the case this time. The house has a floor plan that will be good for us as we get older, and we have a lovely back yard that reminds me of a state park. Because of our vast experience in settling in new houses, we were 95% settled after just two weeks.

That brings me to the latest lesson that God has shown me through simple events in my daily life. It started when I finally had time to sit down at my computer after I had collapsed on the couch after a long day of unpacking. In the age of Facebook, many of us express our feelings and opinions online, and that night a young woman who attends my church had stated her views on some subjects, as she had the right to do. However, so much of what she said was in such conflict with Scripture that I had a difficult time reconciling those views with what I know to be Biblical truth.

As I was feeling troubled about her attitude, God pointed out to me some parallels between my house move and the way He works in His children. When we moved to the new house, we had some wonderful friends who brought their vehicles to haul everything. As things came to the house, we put the furniture and boxes in the right rooms. When everything was finally out of the old house and in the new house, then the actual settling began.

I didn't look at my husband first thing and say, "Where is the box with my grandmother's teacup collection?" or "Let's hang some pictures on the wall!" No, these were the last things on my mind.

The priorities were to set up our bed so we could get some much-needed rest that night, to unpack enough kitchen basics to be able to have a snack or a drink, to get toilet paper in the bathrooms, and to locate our daily medications. These things were the most crucial on that first day. As time went on, we finally got to the teacup collection and artwork on the walls, but there was a process of priorities and foundational things that had to come first.

Pastor Michael preached a series called "God's Treasure Chest" about all that God has placed within each one of us that we must dig for and learn to access so that we can operate in the Kingdom to bring others to Christ. He used this Scripture, among others:

"...as His divine power has given to us all things that *pertain* to life and godliness, through the knowledge of Him who called us by glory and virtue..." (2 Peter 1:3).

He noted that this scripture says, "...has given to us..." not will *someday* be given to us. As I meditated on his sermon series and this Scripture, God showed me something about this young lady and all of us. You see, when we are born again, He makes us a new creature and puts within us all things that pertain to life and godliness, but just like in my new house, God must arrange things within us in a process. It's not that all those things are not equally important, but some things are more immediately necessary and must be in place before we are ready to understand and access all the others.

I could not have hung the pictures on the wall before I had all the furniture in place, or else I'd be trying to wrestle a bookcase against a wall that already had my kids' graduation pictures hanging on it. When we see a brother or sister in Christ that isn't living or speaking biblically, we must be patient with the process. God will "hang the pictures" in their lives if they submit to the way He settles them. We don't give them a free pass to sin, but we treat them with love and acceptance and help to disciple them while God is settling their "house," and we hope that they will do the same with us. It's also our responsibility to examine our own "house" to make sure that we are still allowing God to unpack the boxes of all the things He has put within us, not just leaving a big stack of packing boxes in the spare rooms of our hearts with the contents left unused. Just a few thoughts from a tired but happy vagabond, hoping never to have to see another cardboard box for the rest of her life...

THE END?

God's not finished with me yet, nor is He finished with you. I'll keep listening and learning, and I hope you will as well. If He shows you a little "nugget" of wisdom in your day-to-day life, please share it with others. We all need a word from God as we walk this road of life.

If you have questions or comments or want to respond to something you've read here, please leave me a message on my blog's Facebook page or send me an email. Of course, I hope you'll become a regular reader of the blog as well. Thank you for reading and letting me share my life with you.

Facebook: Over the Circumstances
Email: overthecircumstances@gmail.com
Blog: www.overthecircumstances.blogspot.com

Acknowledgments

I want to thank my beautiful family for being good sports about being used as examples in my writing, for teaching me so much about myself, and for just doing life with me. All my love goes out to Paul, Nikki, Josh, Brittney, and Bella.

My husband and I are members of Covenant Fellowship Church of Bristol, Virginia. Two of our church pastors, lead pastor Michael Booker and associate pastor Scott Emerine, reviewed the manuscript to ensure that every thought was Biblically sound and would encourage those who would read it. Your support in this project has been so important to me. Thank you.

I also want to thank Connie Turner, who, as an avid reader of my blog, encouraged me to compile my writing into a book because she just likes the feeling of a book in her hands.

About the Author

Jan Ellis is a graduate of the National Outreach Bible Institute and has led Bible studies in various settings and programs in the churches of which she was a member. Her blog, overthecircumstances.blogspot.com, was the inspiration for writing her book of the same name. The blog has a Facebook page titled *Over the Circumstances*, and she can be reached by email at overthecircumstances@gmail.com. She holds a master's degree in special education from Marshall University and has taught in the public-school system for 36 years. Jan and her husband, Paul, have lived in three states and twenty-one houses. This frequent migration speaks to either her sense of adventure or the state of her sanity. She is the mother of two adult children, and the grandmother of the irrepressible Bella, whose growth and development sparks many of the stories she shares.

Coming Soon

Jan is currently working on her next book, *Living in the Land of If*, which explores the challenges and lessons inherent in life in general and in her personal story of experiencing a long season of uncertainty about significant life decisions. The story of her evolving, multi-generational household and balancing the needs of five family members is both humorous and thought-provoking.

www.ingramcontent.com/pod-product-compliance
Lightning Source LLC
Chambersburg PA
CBHW031317160426
43196CB00007B/567